This is the most readable book I have held in my hands for many years. It is a page turner, a book without cliches, full of pathos as well as humor – I chuckled aloud often as I read some of it, and also had a lump in my throat as I read other parts, quite un-put-down-able. Here is a golden chain of brief chapters, all linked together by the author's trust in the goodness of God as well as her mighty love for her late husband Anco. One senses that Another's hand was constantly on Christine's hands as she wrote these encouraging sentences. May the same hand be upon everyone who takes this book and reads it.

Geoffrey Thomas
Retired pastor, Alfred Place Baptist Church
Associate Editor, Banner of Truth Magazine, Wales, UK

This is a tender, personally intimate and nearly 'sacred' book by our friend Christine, a well- known author, written as short meditations of sober reflection shortly after her dear husband Anco passed away from a massive stroke following more than five decades of a blessed marriage. It is a book full of the ups-and-downs of mourning and will be a great blessing for mourners, but it is also a book of depth that will plunge you into self-examination and drive you to Christ.

Joel R. Beeke
President, Puritan Reformed Theological Seminary
Grand Rapids, Michigan

I hope the writing was as helpful and healing for Christine, as it was helpful for me in dealing with the recent loss of my father and mother. I think it will benefit others too, and they too will be *Upheld*.

Al Bezuyen
Pastor, URC Sheffield, Ontario

Christine Farenhorst is best known as a writer of vividly gripping, carefully researched historical (Christian) novels. *Upheld* is no less vivid and gripping – even occasionally humorous – but it differs in that it invites the reader into the author's very personal recollections of a devoted and dearly loved husband, as well as of her grief, loneliness, and occasional questions, following his death from a stroke after fifty-three years of a God-honouring and deeply enriching marriage. Vignettes of marriage and family life are interspersed with biblical reflections on God's unfailing goodness, Christian witness, and the hope of heaven. Clearly and unsurprisingly for a natural writer, the process of putting thoughts into print gives evidence of having been therapeutic in itself, but more importantly, what comes through most strongly is an abiding faith and trust in a heavenly Father who makes no mistakes and truly has His children's good at heart. Christine's expressed desire is that others, especially those who are themselves grieving, may be blessed by 'the remembrances of this book.'

J. CAMERON FRASER
Author and retired pastor, Lethbridge, Alberta

This accounting will undoubtedly cause widows and widowers to reflect on their own past journey. It is obvious that Christine grieves deeply, but she does not do so without hope. These pages point to the fact that life on this earth may be short BUT eternity is unending!

WILMA GRINGHUIS
Hamilton, Ontario

Christine has written an insightful memoir of their lives together. I recommend it for widows who know the grief of separation from a beloved spouse and wish to know the sweetness of God's love and presence with them. Beyond widows, I recommend *Upheld* for newly married couples who wish to bring glory to God in the day-to-day of their busy lives.

JACQUELIN SPEAR
Walton, New York

I was greatly blessed by reading this book. There is grieving and rejoicing at the same time of a life well-lived together; of acknowledging the reality of death and separation, the pain and the disappointment, and the struggle to go on without that special someone beside you. It was therapeutic to read it.

ARLENE WASSINK
Lynden, Ontario

This book has universal appeal as a story about faith and loss as Christine mourns the death of her husband while celebrating their life together. What a joy to read!

NATHAN BRUMMEL
Professor, Divine Hope Reformed Bible Seminary, Danville, Indiana

UPHELD

A WIDOW'S STORY OF LOVE, GRIEF & THE CONSTANCY OF GOD

CHRISTINE FARENHORST

paperback ISBN 978-1-5271-1200-1
ebook ISBN 978-1-5271-1287-2

10 9 8 7 6 5 4 3 2 1

Published in 2025
by
Christian Focus Publications Ltd,
Geanies House, Fearn, Ross-shire,
IV20 1TW, Great Britain.

www.christianfocus.com

Cover artwork by Karlee Rene Bowlby
Cover design by Rhian Muir

Printed and bound by
Bell & Bain, Glasgow

Dedicated to the Rock of Salvation

As you come to Him, a living
stone rejected by men but
in the sight of God
chosen and precious,

you yourselves like living stones
are being built up as a spiritual house,
to be a holy priesthood,
to offer spiritual sacrifices
acceptable to God through
Jesus Christ.

For it stands in Scripture:
"Behold, I am laying in Zion a stone,
a cornerstone chosen and precious,
and whoever believes in Him will not be put to shame."

1 Peter 2:4-6

For My Children, Grandchildren and Great-grandchildren

Emberlee and Russell Koning
Matthew and Kristen and their baby Gemma, Emma and Sam and their baby Bo, Stephanie, Marcus, Alex and Ainsley and their baby James, Beatrice, and William

Elineke and Scott Wilkinson
Nathan and Belle and their baby Remi, Ezra and Natalie and their baby Adah, Marco and Keturah and their baby Apollos, Judah and Gabe and their baby Scotty, Keziah, and Tirzah

Christopher and Melissa Farenhorst
Eleanor, Brenna, Edmund, Timothy, Hope, Bethany
Emily and Joseph

Charity and Greg Bylsma
Zoe, Geoffrey, Noelle and Sophie

Benjamin and Karina Farenhorst
Havilah, Jubal, Clement and Natasha

May God uphold all of them!

Prayer

Am I Job that I could say,
If my God took all away,
So that nothing was the same,
Praised be God, praised be His name?

For my husband makes me whole,
And my children fill my soul,
Each and every single day,
God, my God, would I still pray?

In the simple I delight,
In the sun and in my sight,
Should my vision then grow dim,
Would I still bow down to Him?

If a cancer did appear,
Not benign, malignant here,
If my bowels tainted grew,
God, my God, what would I do?

****

All these things You gave to me,
I possess them fearfully,
Were perhaps the error less,
Did I not so hard possess?

Oh, my God, I pray to be,
More like Job – no, more like Thee,
For nothing remains the same,
But Thy name, God, but Thy name.

Christine Farenhorst

Contents

PART III: REACHING OUT – REACHING IN

PART IV: CONTENTMENT IN GRIEF

PART V: EYES ON THE HORIZON

Introduction

At the onset of December 2022, I sent out a letter to my siblings and to my friends which read:

> I don't know how to begin this note. This very day, actually only about seven hours ago, my beloved Anco died. He had a massive stroke last Thursday evening. He was in hospital three and a half days and we, five children and spouses, (except for Christopher's Melissa), were all able to be there. Having lost the ability to speak, Anco was only able to communicate by blinking his eyes. I was with him continually. There was such a struggle with breathing. The evening before last, he was awake and his eyes met mine but they also looked up beyond me – looked at something I could not see. It was the Lord. I knew this and told him that it was fine to go home, that Jesus was waiting and would carry him like a lamb in His arms.

Anco and I had just spoken, the very day he had this stroke, of who would die first.

"I hope you die first," he said to me, "because who would take care of you if I die first?"

I responded, "No, I hope that you die first, because who would take care of you if I were not there?"

We both grinned and thought it might be best if we passed on together – at the same time.

And then God spoke.

I have just come home from the hospital. I had to leave Anco's body behind. I had slept close to that body for the last few days on the hospital bed – holding him, hugging him, wiping his face and his lips and just touching him continually while speaking to him. Elineke, one of my daughters, and I were there when the Lord took him home. And we saw his soul leave his body. What an extraordinary and blessed experience that is! But, oh, his eyes as they looked at me these last few days.

Every fiber of my being is so filled with pain and yet so very thankful. Shall I take good from the hand of God after a wonderful marriage of almost fifty-three years and not this?

Please pray for me and the children.

Love,
Christine

The Injunction

In Philippians 4:4, (and in Thessalonians 5:6), Paul writes that we should "Rejoice in the Lord always."

It is a given that it is easy to rejoice in good times. For example, it is relatively simple to delight in flowers on a spring day; to feel exuberant while walking on a beach with your family; to exult when you have passed an examination; to triumph when your favorite team wins a game; to jubilate when your fiancé proposes; and to be on cloud nine when someone pays you a compliment. The adverb 'always', however, seems a trifle more difficult to apply.

What about the times we feel physically ill? – the times we lose our jobs? – the times someone insults us? – the times that our children forget themselves and mock godly instructions? – the times a spouse leaves for someone else? Should we rejoice then also? What about the moment we are told beyond the shadow of a doubt that a loved one only has so many months, days or hours to live?

We may conclude from the repeated admonitions of Paul, that God definitely wants us to rejoice in Him always, that is, at all times. Paul, who experienced a number of harsh arrests, was likely in prison when he authored these words. It is said that his last prison, the Mamertine prison in Rome, could have been called "The House of Darkness." According to the Roman historian Sallust, this prison's "neglect, darkness and stench" made it a "hideous and terrifying experience." When Paul was, in the end, incarcerated here in a depressing, dirty, lower chamber dungeon, he did not expect to walk out again as a free man. Fettered, his chains were made of rough iron which rusted with the perspiration of his body, a physical enfeeblement which must have caused him severe pain. The weight of those chains, normally around seven kilograms, was debilitating, potentially rendering the Apostle's limbs useless. His food supply was very likely insufficient. Paul was also lonely, (although never alone), and wrote in 2 Timothy 4:16: "The first time I was brought before the judge, no one came with me. Everyone abandoned me. May it not be counted against them." (NLT)

Neither warmth nor gaiety resounded within these prison walls. From a human perspective we see only darkness, dirt, pain, misery and isolation. Yet Paul, through God's grace, was given the broader perspective of understanding that God had placed him where he was, and that, consequently, this was the best possible place for him to be. He did not consider himself a prisoner of the Romans, although these had interred him, but he considered himself "a prisoner of Christ Jesus" (Philemon 1:1).

Paul positively assures us in his epistles, (and his words are the inspired words of God Himself), that joy is possible while we are suffering. He does this even though he was well aware that from time-to-time God places us in situations which can be considered, from our human perspective, horrible. And during these situations we may drink comfort from His words, that joy is possible while we are in woeful distress and hurting wretchedly. Now we need never pretend that the pain is not there. And we need not pretend that the suffering is a fantasy. But we can be certain that it will not have the last word.

Elisabeth Elliot, twice widowed missionary, author and speaker, (1926-2015), said it well:

> "There is no incongruity between the human tears and the pure presence of Christ. He wept human tears too. Nor is there sin in grieving, provided we do not give way to it and begin to pity ourselves. It is still appointed unto man to die and those who are left must grieve, yet not without hope. Resurrection is a fact. There would be no Easter and no basis for the Christian faith without it. Hence, there is

no situation so hopeless, no horizon so black, that God cannot there find His Glory".

Charles Haddon Spurgeon, (1834-1892), beloved pastor and preacher, often down and depressed, said: “The ultimate aim is not to escape anxiety but to allow it to usher us into the healing presence of Jesus Christ.”

PART I:

PLACES IN THE HEART

1

A Watch In The Night

For a thousand years in Your sight are but as yesterday when it is past, or as a watch in the night. Psalm 90:4

We, Anco and I, married in 1969. It was the 27th day of December and a blustery, frigid day it was. The snow lay thick and white. The trees on the mountain brow across from my parental home in Fruitland, Ontario, were heaps of gusty green and ivory. It was almost as though the prophet Isaiah had been sent an invitation to our wedding and was gifting us with a personal present from God on this first day of our married life. "Come let us reason together," Isaiah's voice rang out for his Creator, "though your sins are like scarlet, they shall be as white as snow; though they are red as crimson, they shall be as wool." My bridesmaids had to push me through the alabaster crust of snow which was heaped on top of the hedge between my father's house and the Fruitland, Ontario church where we were to present our vows before God.

The female section of the wedding party, shivering with the rawness of the wind, crowded into the foyer of the church. There were ten of us crowded into that small foyer, plus my Dad, on whose arm I was to lean as I walked into the sanctuary. The younger girls, little nieces who were aged five and younger, were giggling nervously. As the attendants began walking up the carpeted church aisle in their pretty gowns, there was a commotion at the outside door. My nephew, Louis, whose parents had arrived rather late, had fallen off the stone, front steps of the church. The five-year-old unconscious child was carried into the foyer by his father, and from there taken down to the basement. The flower girls and the bridesmaids, already filling the aisle, were stopped short by an usher – stopped in the twinkling of an eye. My sisters, one of whom was my maid-of-honor and also a doctor, immediately left my side to hurry down to the church basement to see if they could be of any help. My father, about to escort me into church but anxious about his oldest grandson, departed as well. Consequently, no matter that I was resplendent in my wedding finery, I was left alone in the church foyer with the caretaker. He was a man of few words and simply stared at me in mute sympathy.

All this time Anco awkwardly stood in the front of the church next to his brother who was the best man. The faces confronting him from the crowded pews were studying him with increasing curiosity, something which he found very disconcerting. He knew everyone was wondering why the wedding party had suddenly come to a state of immobility in the aisle without proceeding to the front. Unperturbed Lloyd, the organist, softly piped on even as people began whispering. After an eternal fifteen minutes, Anco's nerves became a little frayed. He thought something had happened to me. But then my father and sisters returned to the foyer informing me that nephew Louis would be all right and that his Mom was sitting with him and watching him. The flower girls and bridesmaids, after being nudged by the usher once more, sedately continued their advance to the front. The usher then discreetly informed the organist to manouevre his notes in the direction of Wagner's Bridal Chorus. This he did and I was guided in on the arm of my father. Meeting Anco's eye, I smiled and he smiled back.

Our wedding text was 1 John 4:7: "Beloved, let us love one another, for love is from God, and whoever loves has been born of God and knows God." My father preached well, although I confess I did not listen as I ought to have listened, being constantly aware that I truly was a bride and that my groom loved me devotedly. After the sermon, we sang Psalm

95. Anco and I knelt down together on the kneeling bench even as verse 3 was being sung.

To the Lord such might revealing,
Let us come with rev'rence meet,
And, before our Maker kneeling,
Let us worship at His feet.
He is our own God who leads us,
We the people of His care;
With a shepherd's hand He feeds us
As His flock in pastures fair.

The kneeling down together was one of those pivotal moments, a moment of central importance in our lives, which I will never forget. We didn't really know, Anco and I, what exactly we were vowing as we sang Psalm 95:3. We didn't truly understand the enormous importance and implication of its promising and magnificent words. In spite of that, God was faithful and He did lead us, and He did keep us as His sheep throughout our entire marriage.

Possibly the seemingly long time that the bridal party stood motionless in the church aisle, could be rendered as a moment, as the twinkling of an eye. Certainly in the remembrance of it, the instant seems very small. Yet between the foyer and the front of the church, a distance of approximately twenty steps, lay an eternal, pulsing heartbeat that changed us forever – changed me from a Bride into a wife and changed Anco from a Groom into a husband.

And yet, the strange, spiritual truth is this: that both Anco and myself were the Bride.

Ephesians 5:31-32: "Therefore a man shall leave his father and mother and hold fast to his wife, and the two shall become one flesh. This mystery is profound, and I am saying that it refers to Christ and the church."

2

I Will Say No More

The LORD said to Job: "Will the one who contends with the Almighty correct him? Let him who accuses God answer Him!" Then Job answered the LORD: "I am unworthy—how can I reply to You? I put my hand over my mouth. I spoke once, but I have no answer— twice, but I will say no more."
Job 40:1-5 (NIV)

We were babysitting and relaxing in the living room, watching TV. Granddaughter Tirzah, of whom we were taking care, was asleep upstairs in her bedroom. Elineke and Scott had just returned home and were in another room. Anco suddenly bent forward in his chair and held his forehead in his right hand.

"Do you have a headache, sweetheart?"

He responded slowly, nodding and sitting up straight again, only to fall forward once more.

"Do you not feel well?"

Anco continued to wearily incline forward and backward in his chair, holding his head. I ran for Scott and Elineke.

"Dad's not feeling well. Something is terribly wrong."

They came immediately. Scott called 911.

As I knelt down on the floor beside Anco's chair, I spoke to him.

"Sweetheart, I love you so much. But there is one Who loves you more than I love you. And perhaps He is calling you now. That is all right. You can go to Him."

Then I prayed with him.

All the while, during and after this time, Anco made continual slow motions with his right hand. He would laboriously lift it up and touch his mouth, lower it again only to lift it up again to touch his lips.

"What are you trying to say, sweetheart?"

Although Anco could no longer speak, the intermittent action continued.

Scott said, "I think that he is trying to say that he loves you, Mom."

I have pondered this for weeks on end now. What did he mean? What was he trying to say?

I think I know now what it was. And I am so grateful for the knowledge.

****

When Anco had his first stroke in July of 2020, we initially surmised it was the flu. He was feeling a bit under the weather and we had all had the flu – a touch of Covid-19 perhaps and antibodies were healthy.

But when he began dragging his left leg in the early morning hours of July 17, I knew something besides the flu was going on. A 911 call brought an ambulance carrying two medics.

"Good morning, gentlemen, and how are you today?"

Anco, ever the well-mannered host, addressed them amiably, rising from the couch to shake their hand.

"Please sit down, sir," they responded and Anco obliged.

His systolic blood pressure was a frightening 240 and when they hustled him off on a stretcher out the front door, a door which we rarely used, I said, "God go with you, sweetheart," not really expecting to see him again on this side of heaven. I was not permitted to ride with him in the ambulance, courtesy of Covid fear, nor was I allowed into the hospital. God's mandate in Matthew 25:36, "I was sick and you visited me," was countermanded.

By God's grace, Anco lived. We spoke via telephone internet, could see one another's face, and could read the

Bible and pray together a host of times each day. There are no words to convey the blessings and peace that came from these precious moments.

Eventually I was given permission to visit one day a week. Mondays became holy days, hours which we hugely anticipated, moments like unto reconstructed wedding days. The days between were a mixture of loneliness, sadness and reflection, for my beloved as well as for myself.

Job 1:1 speaks of Job. It also speaks of all faithful Christians, including Anco. Anco had two sons and three daughters whereas Job had seven sons and three daughters. Job lost everything – his property, his health, his children and the respect of the community around him. But he did not lose his Savior. Given insight into God's omnipotence and providence, Job came to understand that God is totally in control – that no matter what He does, it is His prerogative and for our benefit.

The almost two and a half years we were given after Anco's recovery of this first stroke were amazing! They were an added gift heaped on top of past benefits which God had already meted out to us.

There were reproaches with which Anco plagued himself for not recognizing obvious signs of a stroke and acting accordingly. There were also innumerable urgent and loving conversations about eternal life with most of the caregivers and patients with whom he came into contact, both inside and outside the hospital sphere. As well, trailing behind, there were the inevitable 'why' questions – the reasons, the motives and the mystery of God's ways.

And when the second stroke came, the Lord said to Anco: "Will the one who contends with the Almighty correct Him? Let him who accuses God answer Him." Recognizing that God is Almighty, righteous, wise and good, Anco answered the Lord unhesitatingly, "I am unworthy—how can I reply to You? I put my hand over my mouth. I spoke once, but I have no answer— twice, but I will say no more."

Anco trusted the Lord's judgement. Often referring to Job 40:1-5, I am sure that he contemplated in those final moments the greatness of God's wisdom and I am sure that he understood that even in this difficult pain, God would unfailingly do what was right for him and for his family.

3

Beginning

Let what you heard from the beginning abide in you. If what you heard from the beginning abides in you, then you too will abide in the Son and in the Father. 1 John 2:24

The first nine months of our married life, Anco and I rented an apartment in downtown Hamilton on George Street. It was a third-floor apartment and, truth be told, it was located in a rather sleazy neighborhood. My Dad and Mom had given us a car for a wedding present. It had cost all of five hundred dollars, a rather sizeable sum in 1969. As neither garage nor driveway existed by our apartment, we were forced to park on the street. Anco found a note under the little, red Renault's windshield wiper one morning on which was scrawled in large letters: "If you park here again, I'll kill you." We were also privy to gunshot sounds one night and one of our across-the-road neighbors had holes in his ground-floor window the next day. Our Lithuanian landlord, Paul Nukosius, was given to drink, and we could often hear and see him snoring away on his living room couch as we walked through the hall towards the stairs leading to our apartment. Mrs. Nukosius, our landlady, was a hardened kleptomaniac. Occasionally she let us know that she would be visiting relatives for a week or so, but the actuality of the matter was that she would then be serving a small prison sentence for theft. Nevertheless, in spite of their frailties, they were unique and pleasant people and we liked them.

We possessed neither telephone nor television and were the happier for it even though we had to run downstairs every time someone tried to contact us. Paying for furniture on time, (and, therefore, not being in possession of it yet), we had to make do with the furnishings provided by the landlady. These consisted of an old gas stove, a tiny fridge, a threadbare couch, a very creaky bed, and a wobbly kitchen table surrounded by four, cracked vinyl-covered chairs. As well, we owned a homemade desk, (at which Anco could study), several plants, a little washing machine on wheels, and a cast-off pool table which Anco had salvaged during a dump run while he was working for a landscaper during a summer job. Donations from well-meaning family members were always welcomed. We hung our laundry in a musty but very cosy attic which led out to a fire-escape and were blissfully happy.

We lived in that George Street apartment for nine months. Cold in the winter and hot in the summer, it was our home. I could easily walk to my downtown Hamilton job and Anco drove the Renault to McMaster University. The Renault was temperamental and often, to his chagrin, overheated. He would then have to stop at the side of the highway and fill up the radiator with water from a watering can before he could motor on.

Anco completed the graduate program for his MA in Science in the spring of 1970. That summer he began a part-time job with a woman who ran a landscaping business. She was, unfortunately, a lady who had hair on her teeth, as they say in Dutch. Extremely bossy, she had a sharp and unkind tongue. She was unpleasant to the extreme! Whenever it rained, however, Anco was given the day off. Wanting to spend time with my husband, I consequently made an appeal to Mr. Carr, the department head of the insurance company for which I worked. A Canadian veteran, Mr. Carr had served in Holland during the Second World War. He had a soft spot for the Netherlands, and addressed me as his 'little Dutch girl'. In lieu of my holidays, he generously allowed me to take days off when it rained. So Anco and I rejoiced in rainy days.

Packing a lunch of peanut butter or cheese sandwiches, hard boiled eggs, plus some freshie in a thermos, we would drive off to the Buffalo Zoo in NY in our little Renault, crossing the border at Niagara Falls. It was great fun and didn't cost very much.

That summer had its intense and worrisome moments. Upon receiving his diploma, Anco had applied to the Guelph Veterinary College as early as he possibly could. As the summer days drifted by, however, he was not notified as to whether or not his application had been accepted. At the eleventh hour, that is to say, in late August of 1970, he finally telephoned McMaster to ask if his transcripts had been sent on. A secretary bluntly informed him that, due to some clerical error, his application had neither been processed nor sent on to Guelph. Devastated, he visited his old university department head and, at length, the application was still transmitted to the Veterinary College with a letter of apology from McMaster attached. Providentially, that mistake gained him an interview. Even though less than ten placements remained, and even though he was one out of about one hundred candidates still to be interviewed, Anco was one of those applicants accepted as a student of veterinary medicine. We were delighted and rejoiced.

The fact that through a visible error God had nevertheless blessed us, pointed to God's amazing providence.

4

Before the Foundation

... He chose us in Him before the foundation of the world, that we should be holy and blameless before Him. In love He predestined us for adoption to Himself as sons through Jesus Christ, according to the purpose of His will ... Ephesians 1:4-5

Everyone begins before time began. In effect, everyone begins before his mother's womb. How strange and marvelous a truth that is! Even that great prophet Jeremiah must have been dumbfounded to hear God say to him: "Before I formed you in the womb I knew you" (Jer. 1:5). This doctrine of foreknowledge should likewise dumbfound all God's children and they should constantly meditate on it.

The encouragement of God's unconditional love before the womb was something I did not fully realize when I was little. I thought I was my parents' child. The wicker cradle in which I had slept stood in the attic and I heard it creak familiarly when I touched it. I thought that I belonged to my parents and they to me. Convinced that food grew in my mother's cupboard and that 'dropjes', 'Dutch licorice', magically materialized in my father's tweed coat pocket, I was not yet immersed in the totality of God's absolute care over the lives of His elect. Persuaded that my father was a walking library, an encyclopedic source of information, I relied on him for all my knowledge.

Two years after we immigrated to Canada, in November of 1960, when I was twelve years old and in grade seven, the phone rang. It was evening and my Mom was cooking supper in the kitchen. I was curled up in a chair in my Dad's study – a study located in the basement. Now I loved answering the phone. We had owned a telephone in Holland, but the times that I had been allowed to actually speak into a receiver could be counted on one hand. Upon our move to Canada, we had become the rich owners of not just one, but two telephones – one in the study and one in the kitchen. With alacrity I jumped up out of my chair and picked up the black receiver.

"Hello."

"Hello," a crisp voice replied, "This is the hospital in Strathroy calling to speak with Mrs. Praamsma."

I raced out of the study, stopped at the bottom of the stairs and yelled up, "Mom!! Phone for you!"

Then, innately curious, I bounced back into the study, picked up the receiver and listened in at the other end.

"Mrs. Praamsma?"

"Yes."

"Mrs. Praamsma, I'm sorry to have to inform you that your husband has been in a serious car accident. He may not live through the night. If it is possible for you to come to the hospital in Strathroy, I would advise you to do so as quickly as possible."

I hung up the phone and screamed. I screamed loud and long and did not stop until my Mom came downstairs and slapped me. Then I was quiet.

An elder came and picked up both my Mom and my sister. She was an intern at St. Michael's Hospital in Toronto and Mom thought she would be a help. They disappeared into the elder's car and drove off into the night, but not before my Mom had softly told me, chucking her hand under my chin, that I was to take care of the house and that she was counting on me.

There was an older lady, a Mrs. Smit, who stayed with us that night – stayed with my sixteen and eighteen-year-old brothers and myself. She was a jolly, rounded lady and fried eggs for breakfast the next morning. Then she went home.

My Father, after an almost year-long stay in the hospital, with a few home-visits to our Willowdale residence in between, eventually recovered. My Mother boarded at the minister's home in Strathroy for most of the duration of his illness. On weekends, my brothers and I were often driven by kind congregation members to Strathroy so that we could visit our Father. During the week, however, we were alone.

Although I had been taught the gospel from the time I was laid into my wicker cradle, I began reading the Bible seriously and personally during this time. Before I went to sleep each night, propped up by my pillow as I read Scripture, I fully came to realize that God was to be depended on, and I started to understand that He was there even when everyone else was gone.

It was not until much later, though, that I also comprehended that my Father's accident had been planned by God – and was working for my good.

5

The Lord Establishes His Steps

The heart of man plans his way, but … Proverbs 16:9

In September of 1970, Anco having been accepted into the College of Veterinary Medicine at Guelph University, we moved to that city. Acquiring a small apartment on MacDonnell street, our lodgings were directly across from the steps of the Church of our Lady on one side and the local pub on the other. Because we were not allowed to park on the driveway of the complex we were renting, we took the liberty of visiting a neighbor who had a very large driveway – the resident priest at the Church of our Lady. Ushered in by a housekeeper and shown into his study, we were seated across from him as he sat at his large desk. A friendly and black-robed man, the priest treated us courteously. As we explained our parking predicament, he nodded thoughtfully. When we eventually came to the point, asking if we might park by the church, the man graciously permitted us use of the church parking lot for as long as we needed it. No theology was exchanged and we rather presumed that this kindness was a good work for him.

The rent for our reddish-brown, brick apartment was ninety dollars a month and we were devastated when Angie, our landlady, raised it to ninety-three dollars two years later. Each morning, after trudging up the steep cathedral steps to reach our car, we drove to the University of Guelph – Anco for his veterinary classes and I for my secretarial duties at the Department of Political Studies.

A mason jar featured prominently on our kitchen counter. Nickels, quarters, dimes, and, yes, pennies which were still alive then, were carefully deposited into that jar. These were the hard-earned wages for the numerous papers I typed up for university students. Woe betide poor Anco if he reached into the jar and then visited Harvey's for a hamburger. I charged twenty-five cents a page and these pages paid the rent each month. The student loan, for which Anco had applied and which he had received, payed for food and gas. Bi-weekly visits to our kind-hearted parents were vital for they supplemented us with cheese, cookies, chocolate bars and other delicacies which we could ill afford. We were blessed.

A little grocery store was situated around the corner of our apartment. It was run by a jolly, rather heavy-set, and greasy-haired Italian. Five dozen pee-wee eggs could be purchased here for a dollar. Those eggs took us through many meals. A lively talker, Giuseppe would lean on the counter and speak to me emotionally about his dear, departed wife.

"We went dancing every Friday," he would tell me, "and I still remember holding her in my arms as we floated around the room. She was a wonderful dancer."

I would nod, my eyes on the eggs and the reduced loaf of bread he held in his hands, and, encouraged by my silence, he would continue.

"One day she felt a lump in her breast. She went to the doctor and he said it was cancer. She had an operation, and then she was gone. All in the space of a few months."

Then he would begin to cry, tears literally rolling down his flabby cheeks onto the egg carton, and I would feel tears welling up in my own eyes as well. The stories he told me, much along the same genre each time, were embellished at each visit. I felt a great tenderness for the big, hulking, grieving Italian. How sad it must have been for him to lose his wife so abruptly. Newly married myself, compassion for his grief sprang up within me whenever he broached the subject. Then I began to notice a myriad number of little black-haired children running and crawling around the store. Barefoot and cute, but with streaks of dirt on their faces, they peered at me from behind boxes and the countertop.

"The children?" I ventured, during one purchase.

"They're mine," he said, as he bagged some apples.

"Yours? But your wife?"

"These are mine with my second wife."

He stopped and rang in my eggs and apples with one hand, swatting one of the kids who had gotten too close to him, over the head with the other hand.

"Get out of here," he threatened, and the child ran, ducking under the counter a safe distance away from parental authority.

"I really miss my first wife," he conversationally added, as he handed me my bag of groceries.

In the doorway behind him, a doorway which led into his home, I saw for the first time, a dark-haired woman. Tall like Giuseppe, she, like the children, was unkempt and quiet. As she blankly stared out at the shelves of food in the store, I smiled at her but she turned away, disappearing back into their apartment.

Perhaps Giuseppe and his wife and children were part of the flock of the Church of our Lady. I don't know. I cannot, to my shame, ever remember asking him what he believed, or if he knew about the blessings of knowing the Lord Jesus. Yet God allowed us to be blessed through Giuseppe's eggs.

James says in chapter 4 of his book, "You do not know what tomorrow will bring. What is your life? For you are a mist that appears for a little time and then vanishes." Perhaps, like many other young couples, Anco and I sometimes unconsciously lived as if we held sway over our future. Between the business of learning, working and laughing, we thought little of the temporariness and the fragility of our lives. We often neglected the precept that only God knew and held the hours between Guelph and heaven; we often forgot that our every moment, our every single movement, was dependent on God's grace.

6

Surrounded

Therefore, since we are surrounded by so great a cloud of witnesses, let us also lay aside every weight, and sin which clings so closely, and let us run with endurance the race that is set before us. Hebrews 12:1

There in one corner of my room she sits – the widow of Nain. And she smiles at me. "Remember the goodness and kindness of the Lord," she says, "How He pities the widow and how He has power over death." And I remember – remember and understand this more now than when Anco was alive.

I know for a fact that in the past I have been negligent in discerning grief and in caring for those who are alone.

There was a widow I knew a long time ago and she was a sour lady, so I thought. She was a woman who, in a most hurtful fashion, pushed away from those who tried to help her. It was a challenge to love her, porcupine that she portrayed. When I told her, perhaps too glibly, that the Lord was especially near widows, she answered, "And will He put His arm around me at night? Will He?" I was too green, too naive to answer positively. Shocked at her words, I kept quiet. But I knew it wasn't true.

But did I really? For if you know something is true, does that truth not rise to your lips from your heart like a waterspout? If you really believe something, can you stop the words that bubble up?

The parents of 'Talitha cumi' sit in another corner of my room. "Listen to the mourners," they whisper, "Don't they know they've no need to weep. Our child opened her eyes and was fed. She got up from her bed and walked about." Consequently, I am reminded by these shadow parents that Anco, who was unable to eat or drink, is now being fed on the mountain of the Lord. I recall by their whispers that he is alive and that those who mourn without hope have no knowledge of the path of life.

Elisha stands in yet another corner of my room. "Remember," his voice encompasses me as he speaks while he leans on a staff, "how I stretched down on the child of the Shunammite woman and the child lived. It is ever so that believers are given life."

There was the moment in which I also fell upon my dead husband's body. It was still warm then – his fingers still flexible and firm. But gradually the coldness of death set in. And, unlike Elisha, who was enabled by God, I could not bestow the gift of life on my dear one. But One greater than Elisha had already carried Anco's soul away – away to heaven.

The widow of Nain's son, Jairus' daughter, and the child raised through Elisha, greeted Anco's entrance into heaven with laughter and joy. "Welcome," they said, "for now you are alive forevermore."

7

Hope Deferred

I remember the days of old; I meditate on all Your works; I consider the work of Your hands. Psalm 143:5

Hope deferred, Proverbs 13:12 says, makes the heart sick. There are none who grasp this better than those who have hoped for a child, month after month, only to be disappointed again and again. It is a sad thing to see young couples, when first married, opting for time to get settled; opting for the 'security' of two jobs; opting for the 'want' of more things, before they finally think they can opt for a family. Frequently, this family does not happen – often the timeline they have posited is not the timeline which has been designated by God.

The second half of Proverbs 13:12 relates that "a desire fulfilled is a tree of life." No one understands this second part of Proverbs 13:12 better than a Hannah, a woman who has prayed for a little one for a long time and who finds out one day that she is indeed to be a mother.

We had been married for almost two years when we found out that our desire was going to be fulfilled. Suspecting for a week or two that this was perhaps the case, but having been disappointed before, we did not really and truly believe that the rabbit test would prove to have joyous results. It was a test in which a female rabbit was injected with a woman's urine. If the woman was pregnant, her urine would cause the rabbit's ovaries to develop temporary tissue structures. A doctor, or lab technician, could check this out after the rabbit was euthanized.

We were visiting my Dad and Mom in Fruitland, Ontario, at the time of the rabbit's demise. It was December 1971 and yes, we had almost been married two years. Anco was outside shovelling the snow from a small sidewalk before tackling the long, parsonage driveway. I was inside, doing some dusting for my Mom. She was in the kitchen and my Dad was in his study. It's strange how some details stick in your mind. The phone, which stood on the wooden cabinet I was dusting, rang and since no one else answered the ring, I picked up the receiver. It was the nurse from our doctor's office in Guelph. Anco and I had been half-expecting, half-not-expecting her call.

"May I speak with Christine," she said.

"Speaking," I answered, beginning to sweat.

"Your test has come back positive," she went on, and then stopped speaking.

Positive, I thought, and the word appeared to me to be a foreign language. I dared not hope that positive meant pregnant. So I merely repeated the word, adding a question mark.

"Positive?"

I stroked the colorful runner on top of the cabinet next to the phone. My Mom had made the runner and it felt warm underneath my fingers.

"Yes, positive. And the doctor would like to see you for a check-up sometime in January."

"You mean I'm ...."

I let the sentence dangle overtop of the runner.

"Yes, you are pregnant. There's no doubt about it."

"Are you sure? I mean ...."

Again I could not finish the sentence.

"Yes."

Her answer was short. No doubt she had more work to do, possibly more phone calls to make.

"Thank you."

I half-croaked the words, meaning to say, 'Thank you for the phone call', but the sentence would not come out in its entirety because of the thickness in my throat. And, oh, there were no words to describe the thanks I felt welling up inside me to God. Tears had begun to course down my cheeks.

Walking over to the window, I tapped on the pane. The tears were still running down my cheeks. Anco turned around at the sound, leaning down on his snow shovel. Studying me for a long moment, he raised his eyebrows in a questioning glance. I nodded and sobbed out loud. His eyebrows went down, his snow shovel dropped, and he smiled. My mother emerged from the kitchen and I told her that the doctor's office had just called and that we were going to have a baby. She immediately called my Dad out of the study and he stood in the livingroom doorway and just contemplated me. All he could say was, "Well!! well!!" repeating the phrase again a moment later, "Well! Well!!"

Anco came in through the breezeway door. His coat collar was turned up and the brown fur of it brushed my cheek as he hugged me in a huge bear hug and then kissed me on the cheek.

"I love you," he whispered, "but I'm going to finish shoveling first."

Sometimes, as believers, we fancy ourselves without hope and we languish for a period. Something "deferred," something put off, can discourage and depress us. Seeing this specific hope coming to pass was uplifting.

My Mom sat me down on a chair and brought out two cups of tea. My Dad, who had gone back to the study, reappeared with a book in his hand. It was a Dutch book entitled *Moeder en Kind*, (Mother and Child). He put the book on my lap as I was sipping my tea.

"This book," he explained, with a rather silly grin on his face, "greatly helped your Mother when she was expecting you and your brothers and sisters."

"Oh, Louis," my mother smiled as she spoke, "that's a really old book. They have different books now with a great deal more information."

I laughed tearfully and thanked my Dad. The book became a treasured part of our library and I read it carefully.

When desire is fulfilled, it is a tree of life. Anco and I sat under its budding branches in the months that followed.

Psalm 34:8 says: "O taste and see that the Lord is good! Blessed is the man who takes refuge in Him!" The definition in the dictionary for 'taste' is the following: "The sensation of flavor perceived in the mouth and throat on contact with a substance – as in 'The wine had a fruity taste'." For a Christian this might translate into: "The sensation of flavor perceived in the heart and soul on contact with an event – as in 'The providence of God provides a lasting and eternal pleasure'."

8

Great Is Your Faithfulness

Because of the Lord's great love we are not consumed, for His compassions never fail. They are new every morning; great is Your faithfulness. I say to myself, "The Lord is my portion; therefore I will wait for Him." Lamentations 3:22-24 (NIV)

A famous and popular hymn by Thomas Chisholm, who suffered ill health throughout most of his life, is entitled 'Great is Thy Faithfulness'. Penned in 1923, it is a beautiful anthem and was one of Anco's favorites.

Great is Thy faithfulness!
Great is Thy faithfulness!
Morning by morning new mercies I see:
All I have needed Thy hand hath provided—
Great is Thy faithfulness, Lord, unto me!

This refrain is very dear and personal to me as well because I experience it each day.

Every morning I walk to the chicken coop. After my first few steps onto the lawn, between the backdoor and the coop, I will stop and look up into the sky. Most days I also, at this point, remember the blessing in Psalm 103 when, like the proverbial mailman, I'm about to plod through snow or rain, sunshine or darkness, towards the hen house. David's words fall down and clothe me. "As high as the heavens are above the earth, so great is His love for those who fear Him;" And then I say: "I fear you, Lord" and am happy and reassured. Next I gaze at the place where the sun comes up over the horizon and

I whisper or shout, according to my mood: "As far as the east is from the west, so far has He removed our transgressions from us." Great indeed is God's faithfulness.

These things I did before Anco died and these things I continue to do today. Is the practice different because Anco is now gone to heaven? No, I experience the same mercies as before. Yet the encounters are distinct as well because there is no one waiting for me in the house when I come back with the eggs, no one with whom I can share my thoughts and observations. Strangely enough, however, mercies seem to grow these days; strangely enough, the faithfulness of God presently seems greater in my eyes. Is that because I now feel so much smaller, so much more minute and so much more dependent on my heavenly Father without Anco?

A package with two books and a note arrived in the mail yesterday from a publishing company in Holland. The note thanked me for my writing. Its sentences were woven together into a compliment which expressed the hope that I would continue to praise God with my words. The two books in the package were books I had written which had been translated into Dutch. I was on my way into town as I took the note and the books out of the mailbox. I read the note standing by the road. After I was back in the car and reread the message, I promptly burst into tears. Great is Thy faithfulness – but, oh, sometimes the longing to share the knowledge and goodness of that faithfulness with Anco overcomes me.

Morning by morning: I see little sparrows fluttering about in our bushes and sitting on our clothes line; I often behold huge flocks of geese fly by honking as they journey; I hear coyotes howling in the field at two a.m.; I read funny jokes; and like a Beethoven pastoral symphony, I discern raindrops splattering their music onto the window and the roof. Because I have always shared all of these mercies with Anco, are they lesser mercies now? My heart knows that they are not.

God is forging a stronger and stronger bond with me. Let me not rebuff Him for "He will yet fill my mouth with laughter and my lips with shouts of joy." (Job 8:21) (NIV)

9

Preparations

... so the next generation would know them even the children yet to be born, and they in turn would tell their children Psalm 78: 6-7 (NIV)

It was a providential thing that I didn't experience any morning sickness when I was expecting any of our children. The only 'abnormality' I developed was a strong craving for peanut butter and banana sandwiches, as well as a constant desire for hard-boiled eggs. Also, if I stood for an indeterminate amount of time in one spot, a light-headedness came over me. Nevertheless, I was quite able to continue my job as secretary in the Political Studies Department of the University of Guelph until two weeks prior to the baby's birth. Anco was, at this time, a second-year student in the Veterinary program at the University and carried a full slate of subjects which often required cramming late into the night. In spite of that, he was able to craft a cradle – a cradle fashioned out of an old beer barrel which we salvaged from someone's garage. It turned out to be a most beautiful piece of work until Anco inadvertently took off one of the iron bands around the barrel nearly causing all the staves of wood to spill off. Angie Traplin, our seventy plus landlady, was most gracious in that she permitted us the use of her garage as a woodworking shop, and she and her bachelor brother, John, followed the progress of the cradle with great interest. They had no children in their lives and shared in the excitement we so obviously exhibited.

People are unconditionally kind to you when you are pregnant. They often offer you their chairs, thinking your condition requires you to sit down all the time, and frequently ask if there is something which you would like to have. Neither Reformed nor unReformed, being pregnant is, in a sense, like having a 'get-out-of-jail free card'. If you land in a ticklish situation, it is possible to use your 'condition' to get you out of this situation. For example, no matter at what hour you are tired, you will be allowed to take a nap; if you don't want to play charades, you will be excused; if you don't want to eat your spinach, that will be tolerated. And the list goes on.

In Holland, my mother had given birth to all her children at home and my father had always been right there by her side, (except one time when she delivered a baby all by herself while he was still running for the doctor). During the early 1970s in Canada, however, husbands were reckoned taboo in the delivery room. But Anco stood a chance of being permitted in to see our child being born if we attended pre-natal classes together. So, as eager parents-to-be, we enrolled in one of these classes. There were approximately ten other couples in the class. Companionably we watched a film on childbirth, oohing and aahing at all the right spots; and together we received pep-talks on exercise, nutrition and relaxation. In our third class we were told to select music that we really enjoyed and to listen to it while we were practicing simulated labor pangs. Lying flat on the floor on a blanket, as Vivaldi's 'Winter' or Beethoven's third piano concerto played, Anco, sitting next to me on the floor, would squeeze my right arm softly, indicating the onset of a simulated pain. I would then have to take a deep, cleansing breath and begin to relax my whole body. The woman who ran the pre-natal class, would come along checking each prostrate couple to see if the mother-to-be was thoroughly relaxed. Legs, knees and arms would need to be floppy enough to fall right down again if she lifted them. As Anco squeezed my arm tighter and tighter, my breathing was to become shallower and shallower, using only the diaphragm, and my whole body was supposed to become as relaxed as a bowl of jello. This was difficult and though I don't think I ever totally reached the jello state, I did achieve a sort of pudding-like relaxation before our final class, a class which included a tour of the hospital.

In the pre-natal class we were taught how to walk and not 'waddle'. We were shown how to pick things up properly, not bending over double but bending down through the knees. We were also told how to stand properly – belly tucked in, back straight.

"You. Yes, you, Mrs. Farenhorst. Can you step to the front of the class, please?"

It was not a question. So I stepped out of the group line and lumbered towards the front.

"This, class," the instructor said as I stood next to her, "is a perfect example... (I think I began to smile proudly here, until she continued) ... a perfect example of how not to stand."

As the months crept on, much advice was proffered on what to eat and what not to eat. My father-in-law constantly told me not to use salt, whereas my own father told me to eat more even as he donated pieces of Gouda cheese, hard-boiled eggs and fish. And while I grew in girth, Nixon became president of the United Sates, Pierre Elliot Trudeau liberalized Canada, my mother sent for reliable cloth diapers from Holland, and God reigned supreme.

10

Numbering Our Days

Lord, You have been our dwelling place throughout all generations. Before the mountains were born or You brought forth the whole world, from everlasting to everlasting You are God. Psalm 90:1 (NIV)

We read Psalm 90 tonight, it being December 31. Every year since we have been married, Anco and I have read Psalm 90 into the new year. Only it was not Anco who read it this time – read it with his sure, steadfast voice stopping every now and then to peer at the listeners over his glasses. It was my son-in-law, Scott, who read it. That's because Anco wasn't there. His body lies in the Mennonite cemetery only a few blocks from where I live in Bloomingdale and his soul resides in heaven with the One Who brought forth the earth – the One Who turns men back to dust saying: Return to dust, O sons of men.

To God a thousand years are like a day just gone by. The length of Anco's days were three score and fourteen.

Math was never my strong point. I distinctly remember that I was in fearsome awe of my grade two teacher – a Miss Roelofsen. She always wore the same black-grey jacket and had a little, silver ornament in the shape of a bell clipped under her collar. She wore thick, horn-rimmed glasses, had grey, bushy eyebrows, and lived with her widowed mother in a poor neighborhood. The hours in her days were heavily numbered with a class of about thirty students who offered her little encouragement.

One day Miss Roelofsen passed out sheets filled with addition and subtraction problems – rows upon rows, and columns upon columns of numbers.

"Fill in the answers," she commanded, and I recall staring at these rows and columns and being filled with a horrible terror.

"You can't go out for recess," she went on, "until you are done."

I knew for a fact that I would never leave the classroom and that I was doomed to stay at my little wooden desk throughout eternity. So I cheated! That is to say, without even trying, I filled in numbers randomly – thirty-nine, eighteen, four, five and twenty. The whole page became a fabricated numerical lie, wet with the sweat of my palms. To add to my distress, the principal walked in, walked up and down the aisles while he peered over small shoulders. Ignorantly, I supposed that if the man saw a full page, he would think I was a good, obedient and diligent student.

Today, though perhaps a trifle more adept at adding and subtracting actual numbers, I feel rather hopeless at God's math. More often than not, I tend to fill in days with calculations of my own making. And what a mess there can be when I cipher hours away randomly!! And my prayer rises:

Teach me to number my days aright, that I may gain a heart of wisdom. Have compassion on me. Satisfy me in the morning with Your unfailing love, that I may sing for joy and be glad all my days!

11

Birth

When a woman is giving birth, she has sorrow because her hour has come, but when she has delivered the baby, she no longer remembers the anguish, for joy that a human being has been born into the world. John 16:21

In the summer of 1972, Anco obtained a job with the Grounds Department of the University of Guelph. This was a wonderful blessing because we could continue to travel to work together as well as eat lunch together. We often sat in the shade of the campus trees while we ate our sandwiches at noon or we would walk over to our little blue Datsun, (the vehicle that had replaced our red Renault), and eat lunch in the car. After lunch I would often have a nap in the front seat.

There was frequently an active mother killdeer (plover) speed-walking around on the parking lot. We usually heard the bird before we actually saw her. Ki-deah!! Ki-deah!! We would grin at one another, get out of the car and walk around the gravel car park. Handsome with a rusty, red tail and black-and-white bands around her neck and head, the little bird had built a nest somewhere on the small stones. Feigning a broken wing, she would try to lead us away from the nest, emitting a shrill, wailing 'Ki-deah! Ki-deah!!' It was a piercing sound. Standing side by side and holding hands, we detected the camouflaged eggs. Difficult to see, they had black and white speckles. Although it would only take twenty-four to twenty-eight days for her eggs to hatch compared to my nine months of pregnancy, I felt a great affinity with the protective mother as she ran helter-skelter across the parking area.

It was a warm summer. I had begun knitting that previous December. As the little stack of booties, sweaters, and blankets grew, so did my stomach. Gaining between forty-five and fifty pounds, I felt there was much more to me than met the eye. Although I spoke to the baby continually, and she kicked fiercely in response, it was still challenging to imagine that a little, flesh-and-blood baby would actually occupy the beer barrel before too long. But on Sunday, August the fifteenth, we definitely knew that something was up, or rather down. We were also extremely thankful that it was a weekend. After all, Anco was home and by my side. What a relief that was to me! But aside from a heavy, low backache, and intermittent pains, nothing happened – even though we stayed up all night, nothing happened! The doctor told us, the next morning, that we ought to check into the hospital by supper time and that I ought to eat nothing for supper. Anco went to his landscaping job, poor fellow, with rings under his eyes. And that evening we checked into the hospital.

After registration and an enema, (from the last two letters in that miserable word, I have surmised that an enema must be a Frisian procedure), a nurse confirmed that I was without any doubt, in labor. At this point I had somehow begun to doubt that I was actually pregnant, so I was quite happy to hear her confirm the fact. Anco was finally allowed to join me after I was installed in a labor room. He looked a little nervous. I assured him that I was fine and so I was for the rest of that evening. We had brought along a book entitled *The Joys of Yiddish*, and Anco read me jokes, talked to me, prayed with me and we had a relatively peaceful time of it. As a matter of fact, the obstetrics nurse who was in and out of our room, joked that I might be one of those unusual mothers who give birth with relative ease.

Our doctor came in to check me around midnight and Anco was asked to leave the room. A tall, thin man with a pale complexion and a wispish smattering of reddish hair, he did not envelop me with confidence. Blue-eyed, as well as slightly cross-eyed, he peered at me from the foot of the bed after he had examined me. The nurse, who had become an exceptionally close friend by this time, held my hand throughout the entire procedure.

"Well, Christine," the doctor informed me, "I'm going to break your water."

The nurse squeezed my hand very hard but said nothing. The doctor then produced a mile-long needle out of nowhere and without wasting any more words, proceeded to break my water. (A few years later this man was convicted of molesting female patients and his license was revoked.)

As he was leaving the room, he commented to the nurse, "This one will be an all-nighter."

It was a very uncomforting thing to say and to hear, but I did not have much time to reflect on it. The next eight hours plus were hard work. It was what my mother had told me when I had asked her what labor was like.

"It's hard work, Christine. Just plain hard work and you have to roll up your sleeves and do it."

Well, I couldn't really roll up my sleeves. The hospital gown was far too short. But I did remember the breathing exercises and with Anco's proficient and tender help, became as relaxed as I could. My poor husband was so weary. It was the second night straight that he was not getting any sleep. Yet the words: "Weeping may tarry for the night, but joy comes with the morning," (Ps. 30:5), flowed around us in a joyous refrain. At approximately 8:20 the next morning, little Emberlee Kristin lustily sang her way into the arms of her smiling and adoring father and mother.

From the labor and delivery room I was wheeled into a ward – a ward which three other mothers already occupied. Snug in a corner, I considered myself blessed to be next to a window. I had seen and held the baby for a moment, but had not really studied her closely as yet. When a nurse brought her in to me a bit later, I was absolutely amazed. Actually, amazed is too small a word. I had the feeling that, through

God's help, I had achieved something which nobody else in the whole world had accomplished before. Little Emberlee was incredibly beautiful!! And although I thoroughly believed the doctrine of 'conceived and born in sin', I was at that moment convinced that she was perfect. Anco totally agreed with me before he went home to sleep. Then the nurse took the baby to the nursery and I also drifted off to sleep – a wonderful sleep – a sleep in which I conquered both Mount Kilimanjaro and Mount Everest and had energy to spare.

Proverbs 22:6 says: "Train up a child in the way he should go; even when he is old he will not depart from it." Grace for parenting would be provided to us in large measure. Left on our own we would not have been able to obey God's command to train up our little girl, and our later children, in the way they should go. God never gives a command but He gives the grace to obey it alongside that command. That part of our children which became dearest to us was their souls, and it became our habit to pray for them each and every single day.

12

Goodness

The fruit of light is goodness, righteousness and truth Ephesians 5:9

Yesterday was Sunday and the first of January 2023. I attended church for the second time without my beloved husband. It would have been my father's 113th birthday. But now he, like Anco, is out of time. People were very kind in church. Three grandchildren – Jubal, Geoffrey and Natasha – sat with me as I occupied Anco's place. A friend came and talked to me. She cried and crying is so very infectious right now, so I cried too.

Today, Monday, I read all of Anco's notes on John 18. He was so very thorough. It was as if he were explaining Scripture to me, as he did most days when I had questions – and the reading of his notes was very comforting. Only his handwriting was so bad – at times almost illegible – and, strangely enough, I found that irritating. I wrote out the notes for Sam, a fine gentleman in church, a man who has graciously agreed to continue to facilitate the Bible study which Anco led. It will be difficult to have a Bible study without Anco. But he remains present through his past professed faith, and that is good.

Even as the Hebrews 11 group, people remain in your heart through their obvious faith and through righteous acts they accomplished – sincere and good acts which are godly.

By faith ... my Mom always got up in the morning before I did and made me breakfast – pea soup, bean with bacon soup or porridge; by faith ... my Mom knitted me sweaters, bought me cosy nighties and always asked how my day at work had gone; by faith ... my Dad taught me to enjoy fine classical music and constantly pointed out God's goodness in the composing of beautiful harmony; by faith ... my Dad stood up, and, consequently, taught me to stand up as well, for solid biblical truth; by faith ... Anco held my hands and prayed with me and for me; by faith ... Anco continually pointed me to Jesus; and by faith ... Anco's eyes shone with indelible love for me and for his Savior.

Hebrews 11 tells me that I am surrounded by a great cloud of witnesses. Three of the dearest people I know are in that cloud.

Such goodness!!

13

Hazel

But godliness with contentment is great gain, for we brought nothing into the world, and we cannot take anything out of the world. 1 Timothy 6:6-7

We survived the financial hardships, Anco and I, mainly due to the generous graces of our parents whom we frequently visited. Coming home from weekends with them, we were usually loaded down with all types of foods.

Little Emberlee Kristin grew, loved sucking pickles and was the apple of her father's eye. She was a visible miracle. My mother had brought me a set of cloth diapers from Holland which were washed in my small, portable washing machine. It rolled on wheels, had a hose which attached to the tap and stored away nicely in the closet directly under the stairs. During that first fall of 1972, I discovered that there was a small clothesline on the lawn kitty corner to our side-door. The lawn belonged to the owner of our housing complex, so I presumed I could make good use of it. And so I did. Diapers, little shirts, nighties, and what have you, blew in the breeze every other day and I often stood back proudly just to watch the fruit of my laundry suds.

One day, however, just as I was hanging up some socks, a door to the apartment directly behind the lawn opened and a woman walked out. I didn't pay any attention, focusing mostly on the laundry and dwelling on the fact that the weatherman had predicted rain that evening.

"Watcha think you're doing?"

The voice was loud and shrill and not at all friendly. I didn't really think it was addressed to myself and only peeked at the woman out of the corner of my eye.

"Hey, you over there. Watcha think you're doing?"

There was no doubt. The voice was directed at me and it was not a happy voice.

"I beg your pardon?" I half-said, half-yelled, a clothes-pin in my hands.

The figure was not too close but I could detect animosity hanging heavily between us, almost like a sheet that had not been wrung out properly.

"Dontcha know other people have to use the clothes line too. You..." and there followed such a barrage of foul language that I dropped the clothespin.

"I'm sorry," I yelled, "I didn't know."

Bending over to pick up the clothespin, I sensed the woman was coming closer. I wondered if she possessed a weapon.

"Take them clothes off the line. It's my turn."

Wordlessly I complied with her directions. Pulling the diapers, the nighties and socks off the line, one at a time, my hands were shaking. And all the time I could hear the woman muttering, hissing, as it were. In no time, my laundry basket was full of damp clothes and I walked over the lawn, back to the stairs, onto the driveway, to our side-door. Glancing over my shoulder, I could see that the woman was standing by the clothesline, hands on her hips, watching me. I shut the door, locked it, and hung the clothes on our portable clothes line in the kitchen.

A few days later, having thought the situation over carefully, I decided that the woman was right. I had been hogging the clothesline. Not on purpose, mind you. But nevertheless, in thoughtlessness I had committed an unneighborly act. I purchased a chocolate bar and resolved to go and visit the woman to apologize, offering the chocolate as a peace offering. It took a few days for my courage to build up, but then one afternoon, as little Emberlee was having her nap, I retraced my steps and went to call on my neighbor. Standing on the patio, chocolate bar in my hand, I smiled apprehensively at the door by which the woman had been standing. Brown with strips of paint peeling off it, it was closed. I swallowed and knocked, but there was no answer. Cautiously I turned the handle and it opened – opened into a hall. Several doors came off the hallway, probably all with separate apartments behind them. I could possibly knock at the first door and see if the irate neighbor lived there. Stepping into the passage, nothing had prepared me for the stench that met my nostrils as soon as I left the patio. It was a horrendous smell. Sour and acrid, it attacked me so that I was forced to go back outside and gulp in some fresh air. Steeling myself, and breathing deeply before I ventured back in, I tried again, once more knocking loudly at the first door on the left. No one answered. I knocked again, but to no avail. Stepping outside once more, I replenished my lungs with fresh air. Then I went back again and tried the second door on the right. It opened almost immediately.

"Hey, I was just thinkin' about tcha."

A little woman, grey thin hair feathering about her bird-like face, smiled at me.

"Thinking about me?" I answered.

"Sure," the little woman said, "I was just thinkin' about tcha."

She was not the same woman who had harassed me about using the clothes-line.

"I was looking," I spoke carefully, "for a woman who lives in this building too. She became rather angry at me last week because I was using the clothesline."

The woman smiled at me.

"That'd be Vi'let. She's not nice."

"Oh," I said, "but I do think that I was using the clothes-line too much. I brought," and here I took the chocolate bar out of my coat pocket, "something..."

I stopped talking. The little woman's eyes had grown big. Her hands reached out and took the chocolate bar out of my hands.

"I was just thinkin' about a chocolate bar," she said.

"Were you?" I asked.

"Yes," she said, tearing the wrapping off the candy with childish rapture.

"Well," I replied, "I hope you enjoy it. What's your name?"

"My name is Hazel," she said and grinned at me.

And one of the scribes came up and heard them disputing with one another, and seeing that He answered them well, asked Him, "Which commandment is the most important of all?" Jesus answered,

> The most important is, 'Hear, O Israel: The Lord our God, the Lord is one. And you shall love the Lord your God with all your heart and with all your soul and with all your mind and with all your strength.' The second is this: 'You shall love your neighbor as yourself.' There is no other commandment greater than these. (Mark 12:28-31)

Hazel was one of the dearest and sweetest neighbors we ever had.

14

Light

While you have the light, believe in the light, that you may become sons of light. John 12:36

As Christians, we are called to not only walk in the light but to be light for others. Light shines in the darkness. The light, of course, is Jesus, the Messiah. He is the Savior and walking with Him we do not walk in darkness. John's words of instruction are meant for all believers in the church of God. They are meant for me also, irregardless of my bleak situation and irrespective of my sad, immediate feeling. I am to walk in the light, to believe in the light and become a daughter of light.

These days in January are short and they are also dark. Strangely enough, there has been a lot of rain – not snow.

It is difficult to tell people that my husband has died. Yesterday our Hindu neighbor who lives a few blocks down the road, came over for some eggs. He buys about five dozen every two weeks. I put a copy of the funeral service bulletin between the eggs. Giving him the carton, I articulated very carefully.

"Ravi, I have to tell you something. Last month my husband died."

He almost dropped the egg cartons and I went into the house to get him a bag. Ravi never wants to come inside. Maybe Hindus are not allowed to fraternize with others. Five dozen eggs are a lot of eggs to carry to the car. But to carry a neighbor's sorrow is even more difficult. He was overcome.

"I'm so sorry," he managed.

Ravi is a very nice man. Just past middle age, he loves his own family very much.

"I'm so sorry, Christine," he repeated as he lifted the eggs into the plastic bag.

"It's all right," I answered.

And then I amplified more on the subject because I wanted to explain and radiate Jesus' love; I wanted to expose him to the light.

"Anco is in heaven you know," I went on, "That's because he believed in God and he believed that God's Son, the Lord Jesus Christ, died for his sins. I will see Anco again because I believe that too."

I swallowed, a bit overcome. Ravi nodded. Then he left, cradling the eggs very carefully.

Later his daughter-in-law Angelica, a white girl who converted to Hinduism, emailed me.

"We are all sorry about your husband," she texted.

And because my light also had to shine before Jessica, I texted her back the same message I had given her father-in-law.

"Anco lives. He is in heaven with His Lord and Savior and I will see him again."

15

Strangers

Do not neglect to show hospitality to strangers, for thereby some have entertained angels unawares. Hebrews 13:2

That very first time I met Hazel, she immediately invited me into her room for a visit. That's all there was to her quarters, just a dingy, single room. It contained a cot-like bed, a chair, a table, a fridge, a sink, peeling wallpaper and a bad smell. As a matter of fact, that smell was so bad it was nose-pinching! Hazel had lived in that room, she told me, for a long, long time. She did not know the number of years. I understood that she received a welfare check and that most of the money from that check went towards the rent. The rest of the money went towards food. There was a half-eaten can of pork and beans peeking at me on the table.

Hazel wasn't sure how old she was. But she did remember one crucial recurring event in her childhood.

"My father used to sing to me," she would say over and again each time I visited.

Hazel also had a friend of sorts who lived in another one of the rooms down the hall. This friend was a tall woman by the name of Andy. Actually her name was Mrs. Anderson, but upon being introduced, Mrs. Anderson told me that all her friends called her Andy. Andy's room was a little bigger than Hazel's room, and she also seemed more mentally alert. She told me that her husband had been a prison guard somewhere in the United States and that he had died just before his pension had come into effect. Hence Andy was also poverty stricken.

Hazel and Andy came over for supper a number of times, that winter of 1972-73. Seated at the kitchen table, they relished every meal, no matter what it was. Afterwards I would sit on our livingroom couch with them and read them a Bible story. They loved it, leaned against me like two little children, tried to outdo one another with comments, and quarreled about whose turn it was to hold Emberlee. Two old, little girls vying for attention. If Hazel had to go to the bathroom, Andy would warn me.

"Better be careful, that one pees on the floor."

I have to admit that this worried both Anco and myself. But there were never any accidents. And afterwards, when they were gone, I would vacuum, clean the furniture and make sure that our little Emberlee hadn't picked up any lice.

My mother bought a small fur rug for Hazel's floor. It was white, a rather unfortunate color for a dirty room. It turned black within the space of a week. But Hazel loved it. Without fail, each time I called on Hazel she would greet me with the same words:

"Hey, I was just thinkin' about tcha."

After she informed me of this, her grin, which was huge, would fan out from ear to ear on her tiny face. She was missing a few teeth but her gums gleamed with happiness in spite of the fact that the wind blew through the cracks in her wall and it was downright chilly when the temperature outside dipped.

Luther said: "God does not need your good works, but your neighbor does." Before we left for Anco's internship in a veterinary clinic in New Brunswick the summer of 1973, I spoke to my landlady and asked if something couldn't be done about the general state of the rooms in which both Hazel and Andy lived. She shook her head.

"They're fine, dear. They don't know any better."

So I telephoned Social Services in Guelph. A nurse called on both Hazel and Andy. Afterwards she came to see me.

"You know," she said, "if Hazel ever had a bath, the shock would probably kill her. Her body is just not used to water."

"But," I said, "you'll do something?"

She didn't promise and so we left for New Brunswick at the end of April, telling both Hazel and Andy we would see them again in September.

Upon our return to Guelph for Anco's last year, however, the apartments were empty. (Later that year they were condemned.) When I questioned the landlady, she told me that both Hazel and Andy had been taken to one of the old age homes in town. In due time we visited, and managed to find Hazel. We hardly recognized her. Scrubbed clean, she had metamorphosed into the sweetest-looking little wisp of a woman. Dressed in a grey dress, she was as proud as a peacock.

"Hey, I was just thinkin' about tcha."

"Do you like it here, Hazel?"

She nodded enthusiastically.

"Is Andy here too?"

But she could not register that information, so we had to find a nurse. She told me that Andy, who had cancer, valued her freedom, and had already run away from the home several times. Later we were able to sit down with Andy as well, but her contentment was minimal. The food was good, she grudgingly admitted, but she couldn't go for walks and people were watching her all the time.

Eight months later, we moved away from Guelph to Chesley, Ontario for Anco's first job. We asked our church consistory to call in on the two women. But the truth is that neither Hazel nor Andy were ever paid a visit by anyone in the church.

There is a legible statement written in tomorrow's clouds. Visible to the spiritual eye, it reads: "I was hungry and you gave me food, I was thirsty and you gave me drink, I was a stranger and you welcomed me, I was naked and you clothed me, I was sick and you visited me, I was in prison and you came to me." To those who have eyes to see and ears to hear, that statement translates into: "As you do unto such as Hazel and Andy, you do unto me."

PART II:

MAKING ENDS MEET

16

Clothing

And why are you anxious about clothing? Consider the lilies of the field, how they grow: they neither toil nor spin, yet I tell you, even Solomon in all his glory was not arrayed like one of these. But if God so clothes the grass of the field, which today is alive and tomorrow is thrown into the oven, will He not much more clothe you, O you of little faith? Matthew 6:28-30

I gave away some of Anco's clothes today. It wrenched my heart something fierce. I packed undies, undershirts, and workshirts. He was put into the coffin in his Sunday suit. Brown and faded, shiny with age, it was the outfit he put on with great care each Lord's Day. Afterwards, I always helped him put on his tie which our daughter Elineke had fixed so that he could slide it on over his head. My task was merely to pull it snugly around his neck. Anco meticulously polished his shoes, his brown Sunday shoes, every Saturday evening. Few people have scruples about what they wear when they go to worship God. Anco was very mindful of the holiness of his God and dressed accordingly.

In the hospital Anco had been mortified to be covered with only a flimsy hospital gown. And I could do nothing about it except stroke his hand continually and clothe his ears with words of encouragement.

"I'm right here, sweetheart. It's all right. And God is here with both of us."

Matthew 6, containing the text, "Do not worry about what you will wear," was one of Anco's favorite passages. The verses 25-34 hung above his desk at work and he read them frequently.

As I lay next to Anco in the hospital bed, I tried to shield him with my own body. I tried constantly to wet his dry lips with water. It was so very hard for him to breathe. And yet there was also the constant awareness that his life, so very tenuous during this time, was being hidden with Christ and being readied for glory. I spoke to him of these truths and had the assurance that they warmed him more than any earthly garment.

I was shopping at the mall today – for birthdays coming up. Taking care to avoid men's sections, I nevertheless bumped into some racks touting men's sweaters. There were many 'after Christmas' sales. The racks brought tears to my eyes and I envied women around me who could browse at leisure and pick out items for their loved ones. Even though my loved one is now robed in righteousness, there is that earthliness in me that would still like to give him things, button up his coat and help him with his gloves. There is such joy in giving.

In the second volume of his biography on Martyn Lloyd-Jones, Iain Murray relates a story about two sisters, known as the Misses Spain. They were faithful attendees at the church services held in Livingstone Hall where Dr. Lloyd-Jones preached. These two sisters always sat in the same spot in church – in the middle block, near the front – and were somewhere in their forties. They were pleasant faces to see, always smiling and courteous. But very little was known about them or their background, except that their father had been a businessman and that both he and his wife had died. The sisters were, therefore, orphans.

One Sunday Rev. Lloyd-Jones preached on the parable of the wedding feast in Matthew 22. He stressed how important it was to have a wedding garment and on the danger of being found without the wedding garment. After the service was over, the older one of the sisters came over to speak with him. She thanked him for the sermon, something she had never done before. They continued chatting and she told him that there was another sister, one who had an important government post on the South Coast. Apart from this sister, there was no family. Iain Murray writes:

> ... this third sister was feeling lonely and was coming up to London that very evening to stay for a few days with them. As she was leaving, she turned back and half shyly said: 'Doctor, I am so glad I have on that wedding garment. Thank you', and went out to join her sister.
>
> That night a bomb fell on their house and all three sisters were killed outright. The members of Westminster Chapel were their family at the burial.
>
> The Doctor always felt, after his conversation with Miss Spain that night, that it was of the Lord's mercy that they had been taken together, theirs was such a close relationship. We might have thought it strange that the third sister had come up from the South Coast to join them on that particular night. But, knowing that the Lord is not only "rich and merciful" but also very kind, we will not call it strange. (Iain Murray, *D.Martyn Lloyd Jones, v2,* Banner of Truth, 1990)

The amazing gospel truth is that God, even as He had clothed the sisters Spain with wedding garments, had clothed my Anco with wedding garments. Indeed, God clothed him with better raiment then I could ever have provided. Presently he is appareled in much better attire than his brown Sunday suit and I cannot come close to imagining what he looks like arrayed in full righteousness – beautiful, resplendent and glorious.

17

Traveling

For the cloud of the Lord was on the tabernacle by day, and fire was in it by night, in the sight of all the house of Israel throughout all their journeys. Exodus 40:38

We traveled from Guelph to Moncton, New Brunswick in the spring of 1973 for Anco's internship in a veterinary clinic. Very excited, and stuffing our little blue Datsun to the hilt, we were full of good cheer and hope. Emberlee was about eight and a half months, and was either snugly ensconced in her car seat during the long trip or cuddling on my lap. (This was the age before mandated seatbelts.) I told her stories, sang to her and played games. Everything but the kitchen sink was crammed into that tiny Datsun, including our second little unborn child, one that would, God willing, be born in New Brunswick.

A Christian family who lived in Moncton had kindly rented a fully furnished basement apartment for us, an apartment which was situated not too far from the veterinary clinic. These kind people welcomed us when we arrived, and fed us supper. Afterwards they took us to our new home, settled us in and left some groceries on the kitchen counter before departing. There we were – the almost veterinary couple. We smiled at each other, put Emberlee to bed in her little crib, and danced around the kitchen/living room. This was our very first placement dealing directly with Anco's calling and we were over the moon.

St. Andrews Presbyterian Church in Moncton was the closest thing to Reformed theology we could find. The pastor's resume included the fact that he had attended Westminster Seminary in Philadelphia and this piece of information had satisfied both sets of parents. They had been worried that we would not sit under sound preaching. There was only one service each Sunday and we missed attending a second one.

There were some negative sides to our basement apartment in Moncton, this largest city of New Brunswick. Firstly, it rained almost every single day that summer. Secondly, the basement apartment's previous tenants had let their dogs pee everywhere. Mingling with the continuous, moist smell of rain, the rooms smelled incredibly foul. Thirdly, the landlord was cross-eyed and played peek-a-boo with Emberlee every day. Although the man could not help the fact that he was walleyed, it severely compromised the ease with which I attended his visits. Fourthly, that same landlord had a master key and walked in without knocking many times during the day. Putting all these things together, I became slightly deranged, and we began hunting for another apartment.

We found a wonderful alternative to the basement apartment – one which was located on the third floor of an old stone farmhouse which could only be reached climbing the fire escape stairs. Situated on the outskirts of Moncton, it possessed an incredible panoramic view of the countryside. Notwithstanding the fact that the rooms contained no furniture to speak of, we rented it without any hesitation. The owner, an agreeable old farmer, was willing to donate several lawn chairs, an old kitchen table, and two beds, (one of which was for my mother who would be coming to help me with the new baby). The landlord also gave us permission to start a garden and to foster a kitten which we named Carmichael. It was great!

Often Emberlee and I traveled with Anco to farms in the Moncton countryside. It more often than not poured rain, but we didn't mind because we were together. On one such an occasion, Anco parked the clinic truck at the foot of a lengthy laneway. The path before us was unbelievably muddy. After studying the route with its seemingly impenetrable puddles, he decided to walk to the farmhouse. Emberlee and I watched him carry his big, black doctor's case as he sloshed up the driveway. Emberlee, early talker that she was, cheered him on, patting the window. "Go, Papa, go!!!" She did see her Papa go, especially after a sizeable, bull-like dog came racing out of the neighboring field to our right. We spotted the dog before Anco did and loudly honked the horn to warn him. Turning, Anco became aware of the warlike creature galloping towards him, and he picked up speed. This was not easy as he was carrying the cumbersome, black veterinary case. But run he did and he almost made it to the barn before the mongrel had fastened its teeth onto the backside of his coveralls ripping out a considerable amount of cloth. The farmer, who spoke French, was apologetic. "Je suis profondément désolé – I'm deeply sorry." But the man grinned as he spoke and Anco was not amused.

On another occasion, Anco was called out a little after twelve one night – called out of our warm bed to attend a calving, his very first calving. A trifle nervous, he checked his case, read his textbook, and disappeared down the fire escape. Hours later he returned home and recounted in detail what had happened.

"I did a vaginal exam. Everything seemed to be going well. The calf seemed to be in normal position."

I listened raptly, extremely proud of him.

"The problem was," Anco continued as he sat on the edge of the bed, "that I couldn't quite figure out the head. I could feel it and then it seemed to be somewhere else. The head just wasn't in the right position."

I patted his shoulder and asked, "Then what happened, sweetheart?"

"Well, the farmer was quiet most of the time. He just watched me, and every now and then would begin to jabber away in French and, honestly, I couldn't understand a word he said. I think it was partly because I was nervous and partly because I'm just not good with the 'Chiac'."

Chiac was the French dialect spoken by a lot of the farmers.

"I'm sure you did well," I comforted, "but what happened next?"

"Well, as I said, the calf was in position, the cow was fully dilated, the calf's legs were visible, but ...."

"But what?"

"Well, she didn't deliver."

I felt my stomach. The little one was kicking. Anco often compared me to cows but that didn't really bother me. Only I really hoped my delivery wouldn't be as problematic as this cow's seemed to be.

"Well, you're home," I said, "so she must have delivered in the long run."

"Yes," Anco said rather despondently, "but I did have to call the clinic. Dr. Berthélémé had to come out and help me."

"Oh, that's all right, sweetheart," I tried to comfort, "After all, it was your first calving."

"Yes, and you'll never believe me when I tell you what happened next."

"What?"

"Well, Dr. Berthélémé performed a caeserian and I assisted."

"I'm so proud of you."

"And it turned out to be a two-headed calf!"

I was quiet for a minute before I repeated what he said.

"A two-headed calf?"

"It was a case of polycephaly," Anco's voice was impressive and professional, and he turned to look directly at me, grinning from ear to ear, "that means having more than one head, sweetheart, and such a thing is extremely rare. And just imagine, it was my very first calving."

The baby kicked me again and I wondered if she had more than one head. That was silly, of course. Sensing my thoughts, Anco smiled.

"Everything will be fine, sweetheart."

And it was. It always was. And it always will be – for abundant is God's goodness which He has stored up for those who fear Him (Psalm 31:19a).

18

Things

For from His fullness we have all received, grace upon grace.
John 1:16

Today I went and bought a boxspring and mattress for the spare bedroom. We gave our spare beds away when we moved from Arthur to Bloomingdale. My Mom, after my Father died, moved into the second bedroom and began sleeping in a single bed. She did that until she died. I never asked her why. Perhaps I considered it too personal a question. I wish now that I had asked her – had asked her many things. I'm the same age now that my Father was when he went to heaven. I'm also the same age Anco was when he went to be with the Lord.

I relish the things that were important to Anco, things that remind me of him. His pillow re-enforces my back at night. His empty chair has a dozen or more sentences that call out each time I pass; it projects many phrases that whisper and caress me; and it holds a lap on which I frequently sat. His sandals and his slippers and his boots echo the gait that walked about our house and onto the patio. The blue toothbrush on the bathroom counter is still part of his hand, recalling camaraderie as we simultaneously brushed our teeth. I wear his sweater; I use his hankie; and I hold his pen.

Are such things wrong? Not, I think, if I ascribe glory to God for these bygone innumerable blessings – for these bountiful mercies that were showered on me in the past.

For our August/September holidays we more often than not traveled to Dog Lake in northern Ontario. Staying at a cottage surrounded by lakes and forests, we caught pickerel, pike, and small and large mouthed bass. Listening to the loons call and watching the bald eagle fly overhead, we exalted in the beauty God had given us. During those late summer weeks, it seemed as if we could relax for a small moment from the bondage and sufferings to which we constantly saw God's people subjected. Rejoicing in a fiat creation, we stood on the tip-toes of our faith waiting in eager expectation together with all of creation for the restoration that will eventually come in Christ. Resting under a biblical broom tree as it were, we slept safely in our boat. Upon waking, we ate the bread and drank the water of angels – angels in the forms of Martyn Lloyd Jones and Spurgeon on tape – while parking in weed beds. In spite of the fact that we felt in these holiday moments a little like Adam and Eve, we were fully aware that suffering would remain a part of our lives until the final return of Christ.

I sit next to Anco's memory in church now where he faithfully held the Bible for me with his right hand these last two years and four months. Sunday after Sunday he held it, while we listened to Scripture being expounded. I still sense the feel of his rough, hard and work-worn hand as he cradled mine when we prayed. I recollect farther back how our children sat around us in the pew when they were growing up, and how, in wonderment at God's mercy, we marveled at the fact that He had extended His covenant to them also.

We took great joy in music, and in my heart I retrieve the sound of our voices as we sang psalms and hymns around the piano on weekend evenings, making joyful noises in our rec room. And I can readily evoke the picture of Anco and I kneeling down together every night in front of our four-poster bed before we went to sleep.

These last things, the singing and the kneeling, they were things which Anco so loved – and which he now does perfectly compared to my still earth-bound imperfection. But someday we will praise God together again in a way that will far surpass anything I can hearken back to now.

Rev. Eric Alexander, who died a month after my beloved Anco died, and whose sermons greatly blessed us, said at the funeral of his friend, James Montgomery Boice:

> No eye has seen, no ear has heard, no mind has conceived what God has prepared for those who love him" (1 Cor. 2:9) There is no human language, there is no human word to express it, but because of what it means to depart and be with Christ, which is far better, all we may say today is that "far better" covers everything. It is far better to be in glory than to be here in this world. We will never really understand the full meaning of it until, by God's grace, we join Him. See that you join Him. See that you join Him.

19

But Your Dead Shall Live

Your dead shall live; their bodies shall rise. You who dwell in the dust, awake and sing for joy! For your dew is a dew of light, and the earth will give birth to the dead. Isaiah 26:19

In the fall of 2022, a few months before the Lord took Anco to heaven, I was in the garden harvesting corn. Our plot of corn is fairly close to the back fence and my neighbor came out. I walked over to the steel railing to chat with him. He was in the process of planting garlic. He loves garlic and makes all sorts of sauces out of his crop.

"How are you, George?" I asked by way of a conversation starter.

"Oh, all right," he answered, getting up from his knees.

We discussed garlic extensively – when and how to plant, what kind of manure to use, what to make out of the garlic, and so on – before he suddenly scowled, telling me he had something sad to do that afternoon.

"What is that?"

"I've got to go and bury the wife this afternoon."

I was taken aback because I knew that she had died some years ago. Was I wrong about that?

"Bury your wife?" I repeated his words, somewhat bewildered.

"Yup," George confirmed, "she's been up on the mantel for a few years now and I think it's about time to put her to rest. My daughter and I are going to bury her proper this afternoon."

A light dawned on me. A cremation jar must be adorning his mantel.

"I see," I nodded, "and where is the cemetery?"

"Oh, just around the corner," he replied, "the Mennonite cemetery. But," he added, "it's still a hard thing to do."

"Was she a Christian?" I ventured, "Did she believe in the Lord Jesus Christ?"

He immediately acknowledged that she was.

"She was a Catholic."

"Oh."

I had not known George's wife. He was, at this point in our conversation, obviously in distress.

"If she believed in the Lord Jesus Christ and was sorry for her sins, and if she believed that He died for her and forgave her sins," I added, "then she is in heaven."

"The trouble is," George was quite agitated now, "that the Roman Catholic Church disagrees with her being buried in a Mennonite cemetery because the ground is not consecrated."

"Well," I comforted and reiterated at the same time, "if she believed that Jesus Christ was her Savior and died for her sins, then it really doesn't matter where she's buried, does it? Because she will already be in heaven."

Anco had driven up behind us in his scooter during the latter part of the conversation. He heartily affirmed what I had just said.

"That's what the people at the cemetery told me too," George agreed.

"George, if you also believe in the Lord Jesus and are sorry for your sins, and if you believe that He died for your sins as well," we added, "then you will see your wife again when you die."

"I have a little trouble reading the Bible," George replied, "It's a big book and some people say it means one thing and some say another. How do you know who's telling the truth?"

"The Bible is not so difficult, George," Anco said, "If you read it, and ask God to help you, you will understand what is necessary."

"But what if you don't," he asked.

"Then you come and talk to your neighbors," I countered.

We laughed.

George did come to visit his neighbor. He came to Anco's funeral service in December and clearly heard the gospel proclaimed.

20

Hospitality

Share with the Lord's people who are in need. Practice hospitality. Romans 12:13 (NIV)

After Emberlee was born, we bought an electric typewriter. This was a huge investment but it meant I could type up student papers at home – papers due as semester assignments or papers for students working on their theses. Our rent money continued to be kept in a mason jar on the kitchen counter.

Besides our parents, there were other people who occasionally displayed compassion on our 'poor student' status. One such couple who took a tenderhearted interest in us were a Mr. and Mrs. Pot senior. An older couple who lived not too far from the church, they were rather impoverished themselves. One Sunday they invited us over after the morning church service. After she made us comfortable in the livingroom, Mrs. Pot began puttering about in the kitchen and Mr. Pot engaged Anco in a much-loved game of chess. When Mrs. Pot came back into the livingroom a bit later, she was carrying a tray with four cups of steaming, hot chocolate surrounded by plates of pastry.

"I bought these especially for you this week," she proclaimed proudly, a huge smile on her face.

I smiled back and anticipated enjoying one of the big triangular fruit wedges on the tray, a wedge covered with powdered sugar. Mrs. Pot and I chatted affably about this and that, as Anco continued to play chess with Mr. Pot.

Into the third bite of the pastry, I detected a rather earthy taste in my mouth and suppressed an urge to spit out what I was eating. Surreptitiously scanning the inside of my triangular wedge, I discovered to my horror that it was lined with mold. Mrs. Pot, who saw me look, ventured a modest statement.

"Isn't it good? I'll bet you haven't eaten anything like this for a long time!"

I was only able to nod weakly, and took a sip of the scalding hot chocolate to flush down the mold. It was a moment in which the question, "Do you always tell the truth?" hung heavily over my chair like the sword of Damocles. Anco appeared to be having no problems whatsoever and absently smiled at me as he moved a pawn. I discreetly peered into my pastry once more just to make sure that I had not made a mistake. Sure enough, my eyes had not deceived me. The mold hugged the interior of the wedge like green icing. Mrs. Pot beamed at me again and a patch of sunlight caught a faded spot on the carpet. I knew she considered both Anco and myself underfed, and had taken great pains to buy something special for us. I quickly took another bite of the pastry, washing it away it with a very hot swallow of the chocolate. It was a fact that I suddenly felt strongly compelled to consume as rapidly as possible the green substance hidden within the pastry. The entire wedge disappeared within two minutes from my plate.

"My," Mrs. Pot commented as I literally wolfed that wedge down, "that was fast. Would you like another piece?"

"No, thank you," I croaked a trifle hoarsely, "but it was delicious."

She appeared very pleased with the comment, and I knew that my statement, strange as it sounded to my stomach, was Gospel truth to my heart.

During the second week of our marriage, I concocted a yellow pound cake. It was my first baking attempt and, consequently, subject to trial and error. With twenty-twenty hindsight vision, I can clearly ascertain at this point that my error lay in covering the batter with a plastic lid before I placed it into the oven. It emerged beautifully glazed but admittedly, a trifle inedible. Anco, seeing my crestfallen face, cut a piece out of the shiny loaf and ate it with a smile on his face.

"It's delicious, sweetheart," he said, "but I think I'll leave it at that."

Amy Carmichael said: "You can give without loving, but you cannot love without giving."

Anco loved me very much.

21

Bottle Days and Little Things

You have kept count of my tossings; put my tears in your bottle. Are they not in your book? Psalm 56:8

Today was a day of tears. I wept at almost everything that happened. A Bible text, a painting, a book, the almost-opened blossom of an orchid, the almost-finished sunroom in which Anco will never sit, the hawk that came to perch on the fence, and the cauliflower I cleaned which Anco would have so enjoyed.

What have I learned in this day that now lies behind me? First of all, I learned that it was short – a breath, a whisper, a small cry. I got up from bed only a moment ago and now am ready for another sleep.

Secondly, I perceived that the hours have grown quieter. My voice has waxed inward as Anco's voice has turned still. There is no badness in the silence – only the sounds I used to hear are gone. Anco's breathing, the clearing of his throat, his walk, his sitting down and rising, his singing and his endearments, "And how is my little girl!" and "My sweetheart is looking so pretty today."

Today I came across a note I wrote to Anco years ago prior to leaving for a week or so to help Elineke who was having her third baby. I knew he would miss me, so I wrote him some silly notes, some little notes, hiding them under his pillow, in the kitchen cupboard and in his lunches.

> Dear Anco: I hope you sleep well tonight and I hope that I do too. Maybe you won't find this under your pillow for a few nights. Or maybe you'll look under your pillow because you hope to find a piece of me in bed yet.
>
> Here I am, in the bathroom, sitting on the edge of the bathtub, writing you a note. I don't want you to know because surprises, nice ones, are like someone saying, 'I love you'. And I do love you and hope you will be all right by yourself. Have a good breakfast and think of me.
>
> I hope we see each other again soon, because even though I am still here, I miss you.
>
> Love, your wife, and sweetheart, and friend, and talker, and cleaning lady, and buddy,
>
> Christine

And another note read:

> Ah, you are lonely, you are lost,
> And miss me at the dreadful cost
> Of miles, of distance and of space
> And wish you could caress my face!
> And so I wish you could, my sweet,
> As I would like to tickle feet,
> But I will substitute provide,
> No, not my form, not I the bride.
> But something for your appetite,
> Look in my jewel box tonight.
>
> Love, Christine

I had put a chocolate bar in my jewelry box. These were silly things, little things, but little things are great things to people who love. I came across a small notepad in Anco's desk just the other day. He was always at a loss as to what to buy me for my birthday. Consequently, he had compiled a list on one of the pages of his notepad. The list enumerated presents, (and where to get them), for me in the future. It read:

Red socks – Chapters
Blue teddy bear
Housecoat
Heat socks – Mark's
Potato masher
Potentilla (Cinquefoil) – yellow orange
Gluten-free birthday cake – Farm Boy

Augustine said: "What is a little thing, but just a little thing. But to be faithful in a little thing is a great thing."

Jesus said: "Well done, good and faithful servant! You have been faithful with a few things; I will put you in charge of many things. Come and share your master's happiness!" (Matt 25:21) (NIV)

22

Hearing Prayer

As a father shows compassion to his children, so the LORD shows compassion to those who fear Him. For He knows our frame, He remembers that we are dust. Psalm 103:13-14

Years ago, just prior to our engagement in 1968, Anco and I went to visit an older couple, a couple in their late thirties. Grace and Ernest loved the Lord dearly and spoke of Him often. They lived on a beautiful, little hobby farm on Highway 8 in the Niagara Peninsula. Grace was a teacher and Ernest worked at a steel factory, at Stelco. There was, however, a great sadness in their lives. Although they had been married for almost fifteen years, they had not been blessed with children. Like Sarah, Grace was rapidly approaching the age where it would no longer be possible to have children. When she spoke of this, her eyes would cloud over and often she would weep, not only before me but also before the Lord. She begged Him for children. On her knees she would beg Him over and over, and she would promise to raise up her children in the fear of the Lord. It was a good prayer and one, I am sure, that pleased the Lord.

Ernest and Grace had us over to counsel us to wait a few years before we seriously considered marriage. They were convinced our youthful twenty years were not enough to tackle the complexities of married life. While offering us cookies and Sprite, they fondly urged us to reset the date. Whereas we appreciated their advice, which was lovingly given, we did not heed it and were married a year later in December of 1969.

There was one thing which I left out. Grace's doctor had advised her and Ernest not to have children. You see, Grace had diabetes and the doctor thought pregnancy would aggravate the disease. After Anco and I were married, Grace did become pregnant. She and Ernest were ecstatic. Ernest immediately paved their gravel driveway because he envisioned a little youngster roller-skating on it. Their conversation was now totally colored by this coming child, this coming birth. The sad part was that after she carried this little baby for three months, Grace miscarried. Not only that, but her diabetes became much, much worse. She lost her eyesight. Ernest had to comb her hair, do the cooking and clean the house. In less than a year she was hospitalized and when I went to visit her with my father, who was her pastor, it was difficult to recognize her. The sweet, trim body I had known was puffed up with water retention and she was in and out of consciousness. I wept at the ugliness, the havoc wreaked by sin. Although Grace did not recognize me and died almost a week after my visit, my father recounted that in her conscious moments she testified of her love for God and her desire to be with Him.

Did God answer Grace's prayer?

During the course of our brief sojourn on earth, we pray for many things. Grace and Ernest prayed for a baby. God heard them. After Anco's first stroke, we both prayed that he might still live many fruitful years. God gave us two years, four months, two weeks and four days.

Our lives were salted with 'grace' stories. Reflecting on the different ways we might have perceived them, there are a number of truths Anco and I came to understand. We learned that we might ask God for anything in His name. We came to know that God was not only a God of the major events that happened in the world – things such as wars, famines, earthquakes and economies – but that He was also a God of the minor things in the world – things such as falling sparrows, lilacs and ice cream cones. Difficult as it was, we came to understand that there was no need to pose certain questions. Questions such as: Why is there barrenness in this particular godly household when the neighbor has eight children and does not care for them properly? Why is this Christian mother afflicted with multiple sclerosis whereas the blasphemer is so amazingly healthy? Why does God withhold marriage from this wonderful girl although the atheists down the street are celebrating their sixtieth anniversary? And why does He allow a man such as Anco, who is such a wonderful husband and father, and such a godly influence, to suffer and die of a stroke?

Anco and I never had any doubts that all was well in God's hands. We did not badger Him to reveal to us all His 'secret' reasons for doing things. But we did rely heavily on what He did reveal to us: that His yoke is easy and that His burden is light; that He is a Wonderful Counselor, an Almighty God and an Everlasting Father; that when we walk through the valley of the shadow of death we need not fear evil, for He is with us; and that when our body lies in the grave He will call that body out of the grave at the last day with the sound of His trumpet to everlasting life.

23

Away From Calamity

The righteous man perishes, and no one lays it to heart; devout men are taken away, while no one understands. For the righteous man is taken away from calamity; he enters into peace; they rest in their beds who walk in their uprightness. Isaiah 57:1-2

When my family first emigrated to Canada, we lived in Willowdale, Ontario. John Street, the road on which our house was built, is no longer in existence. It was a small, dead-end street right off the not-so-busy then, thoroughfare of Young Street. If you crossed Young Street at the point where our little road met it, and climbed a path straight up a hill of sorts on the other side, you arrived at a United Church. A cemetery surrounded that church. I often walked there on Sundays with girlfriends. As we ambled between the gravestones, we would marvel at the old, old age of the markers over the burial places and we curiously read the inscriptions on them. There was one in particular which we sought out because it would make us, in our as yet undeveloped faith, laugh. It read:

Since I was so early done for,
I wonder what I was begun for.

Cemeteries hold a fascination for many people, old and young alike. There is a quietness there, a certain air of peacefulness and a leveling of all. When we traveled, Anco and I often stopped to walk around local cemeteries. It was either to sit quietly and eat a packed lunch, or to stretch our legs and meet people whom we possibly might meet again in the hereafter. It was history under one's feet; it was empty bodies without souls sleeping under trees and grass.

Just last year on the way home from a holiday up north, we stopped by a small graveyard at the side of a highway and, after enjoying a snooze in the car, went for a leisurely stroll. One of the gravestones had the curious shape of a clover leaf. We went to inspect it and after reading the inscription, Anco noted that there were some coins lying on the greenish, moss-covered, stone marker. As a matter of fact, there were a lot of coins – toonies, loonies, quarters and dimes. We picked them up, grinned and pocketed the change. Anco suggested we look for another clover leaf gravestone. Strangely enough, there was another clover leaf monument with more change scattered over its granite grandeur. We pocketed that as well, feeling like children who had discovered a treasure trove. As sensible Reformed Christians, we knew for a fact that the body resting underneath the stone, would neither miss nor use the money. We, however, being rather hungry, could do with a burger and fries.

The story is told of an Amish farmer who died in the middle of a harvest season. Because it was such a busy time, the neighbors decided to send one of their boys to the funeral as a representative of all. On the day of the funeral, the boy was walking along the road to the cemetery when a horse and buggy pulled up next to him. The driver invited the boy to ride with him and they continued on their way together.

"Who are you," the boy questioned the driver.

"I'm a preacher on my way to the cemetery. Do you know where that is?"

The boy replied that he was on his way there also and that he would be glad to show the preacher where it was. But after a few moments of reflection, the boy spoke again.

"If you're a preacher, you surely show people the way to heaven, don't you?" he hesitantly supposed.

"That's correct," the preacher replied.

"Then why don't you know the way to the cemetery, when that is so much closer than heaven?"

It was cold when we gathered in the Bloomingdale Mennonite Cemetery to lay Anco's body to rest, to pay our last respects and to recite the Apostles' Creed with family and friends. There was an icy wind that froze the tears on our cheeks and that commingled shivers with sobs. My youngest son put a clod of earth in my hand which I threw onto the casket. The earth was as hard as a rock. Shattering, it broke off in small, compact clumps on the coffin.

"Ashes to ashes, dust to dust...."

Dust Anco was and to dust he was returning. That is to say, his physical body was returning to dust, but his soul was already at home with God. This world was not his permanent home, nor is it mine.

Cemeteries are temporary places, waiting stations, until that time when Jesus returns and our bodies are reunited with our souls.

24

Trust

Why should I fear in times of trouble, when the iniquity of those who cheat me surrounds me, those who trust in their wealth and boast of the abundance of their riches? Psalm 49:5-6

Although we were in some respects materially lacking when we lived in Guelph during those four years of Anco's schooling there, we did lead healthy, well-fed and happy lives. Approved to receive financial assistance, each year Anco applied to the government for a student loan/grant. These loan/grants were designed to help post-secondary students pay for their education in Canada. Required to begin to pay the loan back six months after graduation, it was interest free. The first year Anco applied was 1970 and we received what we perceived to be a rather small amount of money. Consequently, we appealed it. Listing our bills in point form, we sent it in to the Government Student Loans in Canada Department with this note attached.

"We realize you must receive many appeals, but in this small walk of life we are finding it rather difficult to keep body and 'sole' together. And though it is quite embarrassing to ask friends to bring their own chairs when they visit us, it is doubly mortifying to ask them to bring their own teabag. We have, of course, dispensed with our personal maid and valet, but we're rather lonely, just the two of us and all our bills. Perhaps this will explain our situation:

A sweet couple much in l'amour,

Not rich, middleclass, just quite poor,
Sends government plea,
For not much money
But just a little bit moor.

Thanks for taking the trouble to read this appeal."

Surprisingly enough, there was no response.

The year 1972, the year we were expecting our first little baby, I typed out the doctoral thesis for one of the professors of our department. It was painstaking work – work before the time of today's computers which can automatically erase errors. You either typed correctly or you had to redo the page. The margins had to be exact, no white-out was allowed and if even a slight crease or a smudge crowned the page, well, it had to be redone. Theses, however, paid more per page and we were excited to have this little bit of income prop up the earnings in our baby jar. I had received permission from Dr. Melby, the chairman of the Political Studies Department where I was the secretary, to use the electric typewriter in the office. So Anco and I spent many evenings in that office. Anco studied and I worked on the thesis.

When the thesis was finished, and had been presented before the dissertation committee and had passed muster, so to speak, it was time for me to be paid, to be paid a few hundred dollars, a few months' rent. The professor for whom I had typed the thesis, called me into his office after hours.

"Well, Christine," he began, while sitting behind his desk, legs crossed and arms folded, "Well, it's finally finished."

I smiled and nodded.

"So I've decided," he went on, "since you have been using the department's typewriter, and since you have been using the department's office space as well, that I'm only going to pay you half of what we agreed upon."

My smiled faded, my jaw dropped and my heart began to thump.

"What do you mean?"

"I mean that you have benefited from working in this department and that therefore, I don't have to pay you as much as we originally decided."

He reached for his wallet and then stood up.

"I will pay you half the amount," he continued, "and actually I don't have to pay you at all. After all, you work for Political Studies."

"I worked in the evenings on my own time," I responded and my voice shook, "and Dr. Melby gave me permission to use the typewriter and we agreed ...."

He didn't let me finish.

"Half, Christine. Half. That's all I'm going to give you."

"I don't want half," I answered back thickly, holding back tears, "I want the right amount or nothing."

The baby kicked me and I wanted to kick him. He smiled at me, quite sure of himself.

"Well, it's your choice."

"My choice is the agreed upon amount," I returned, suddenly calm, "but someday you will stand before God and then you will have to give an account of what happened."

Then I walked out while the professor chuckled.

Later, I cried on Anco's shoulder. I was convinced that we had to storm the ramparts of the university, that we had to notify the president of the university, that we should sue the university, and that we should devise a host of other tactics which would see justice carried out. Anco, the peacemaker, calmly patted my back and asserted that we should not give Christianity a bad name, that justice is always carried out by God in the end, and that, for the present, we should simply trust the One Who had provided for us thus far.

And he was right. We were never paid the money, but we have never been in want nor have times of trouble ever overcome us.

25

My Heart

For this is the covenant that I will make with the house of Israel after those days, declares the LORD: I will put My law within them, and I will write it on their hearts. And I will be their God, and they shall be My people. Jeremiah 31:33

There was the cleaning up of the bathroom as well as the cleaning up of documents today. I vastly preferred the bathroom clean-up. There had already been a frantic search for Anco's will a few weeks past when, providentially, it was found.

There are many documents: documents which have to do with investments; documents about the car; documents about the house; and documents about the pension. Most of them are Greek to me and I have to steel myself to go through them all. Taxes, warrantees and insurance papers – it's like climbing a mountain of pebbles on bare feet often resulting in a disastrous sliding down towards the unknown.

The chicken coop light has not been working for a number of days. Ordinarily Anco would have looked at it and, in all probability, would have fixed it. But he cannot, (even though the light of his countenance is shining and he is in the city of light), reach down with his arm and fix that chicken coop light for me. So, after fiddling with the electric cord for a few days, I finally had the common sense to unscrew the bulb, take it to the house and insert it into another socket to see if it actually still worked. It did not!! So I got a new bulb, trudged back to the coop and inserted the new bulb. And lo and behold, last night the light worked again. Reflecting on this, it was admittedly very simple. I could hear Anco saying, even as he smiled, "I'm proud of you, sweetheart!" Strangely enough, that brought tears to my eyes.

There are many more concerns, however, than changing light bulbs in the chicken coop. A woman phoned from the Toronto Dominion Bank yesterday regarding a question about the estate. The lady, who was nice but who communicated like a waterfall, had a confusing accent. Every third word was difficult for me to understand. I could guess, but it was a tricky business. Anco always fielded the phone, especially with bank, care or medical calls. Polished and correct, he was sure of himself. Eventually my Toronto Dominion Bank call worked out. "I'm proud of you, sweetheart!" And yes, the old tears sprang into my eyes again.

Prayer figures high in these circumstances. It is at these times that the Lord likes to see me folding my hands – folding them figuratively in my heart even as I'm holding a light bulb or a phone. My help comes from the Lord, the Maker of heaven and earth. For did He not also make the light and my ears and my understanding?

It is easy to forget how close God is to me – especially when I am so full of other things, things which push out the awareness of His presence.

In devotions, while reading Isaiah 30 a few days ago, I was struck by verses 20 and 21. So I've begun to read and reread them and they've proved very helpful and comforting. It is indubitably clear that there have been decisions for me to make – decisions regarding the car, my finances, and just plain, every-day, little decisions that, prior to Anco's death, we always fielded together.

Isaiah says: "And though the Lord give you the bread of adversity and the water of affliction, yet your Teacher will not hide Himself anymore, but your eyes shall see your Teacher. And your ears shall hear a word behind you, saying, 'This is the way, walk in it', when you turn to the right or when you turn to the left."

It's not as if I suddenly am a Wall Street financial wizard, or am gaining a lot of insight into matters which previously seemed dark and murky. It's just that I know within my heart that God will take care of me.

26

Moving

Then Joseph said to his brothers, "I am about to die. But God will surely come to your aid and take you up out of this land to the land He promised on oath to Abraham, Isaac and Jacob." Genesis 50:54 (NIV)

In 1974, our growing little family, that is to say, Anco and I and two small daughters, Emberlee and Elineke, moved from Guelph to the little town of Chesley, Ontario. Anco became the employee of the local veterinarian there. We were earning a real salary – a whopping $14,500 a year – and we considered ourselves millionaires. The contract held the stipulation, however, that I had to answer the telephone at home during the evenings when Anco was 'on call'.

From our vantage point of some forty-five plus years later, if we were to look down on our life in Chesley, and our later life in Owen Sound, we would wholeheartedly agree with James that our lives were indeed like a mist, for those years have vanished quickly. They appeared for a little while and then they were gone.

And yet there are the memories – the good ones and the bad ones.

There were the times in the first few years that we lived in Chesley that Anco would pick me up from home to go with him on a number of calls he had to make. Emberlee and Elineke, who were three and two years of age, would come with us. On one of these occasions we journeyed to one of the many Amish farms in the district. The couple who lived on the farm, Rachel and Amos, were approximately the same age that Anco and I were.

Rachel invited me into the house together with the girls and Anco walked towards the barn with Amos to examine a cow. It was fall and the weather was beginning to turn frosty. Leaves crisped under our feet as we stepped across the lawn. Both the girls had too much energy to sit down quietly at the table in the kitchen. So I let them play outside with the admonition that they stay close to the house.

Rachel had just recently delivered her third baby. It was a little boy. Wrapped up tightly against possible draft, although the kitchen was warm with the wood stove going full blast, he was an endearing little bundle in his mother's arms. I smiled at the picture and seeing me smile, Rachel shyly stood up and came over to where I was sitting on a wooden bench against the wall. She held the infant out for me to hold. I was honored and most willing. Outside, just past the dark blue, almost black, curtains, I could see my small daughters chasing a kitten.

"He is beautiful," I said to Rachel and she smiled.

But even as she smiled, I saw her mouth tremble with a suppressed grief.

The truth of it was that the past spring, just as the ground was beginning to thaw and as the snow was rapidly disappearing, Rachel and her husband Amos had undergone a great sorrow. Early one morning, Rachel, after feeding the wood stove a number of logs, had followed Amos to the barn for her customary chores. When she opened the barn door to return to the house some time later, she was horrified to see her home engulfed in flames. Had the door to the stove been left open? In a matter of less than an hour, her dwelling had become a crackling inferno. Screaming for Amos to come, she ran towards the front entrance, but even before she reached it the home collapsed.

A house can certainly be rebuilt. But even as Anco and I had two small daughters, so Rachel and Amos had been the parents of two small daughters. These were sleeping inside the house at the time of the fire and they were both burnt to death. Buried on the farm, this second house we were visiting, had been built next to two little graves.

Rachel watched me out of the corner of her eye as I dandled the baby on my knee. But I could see that she also watched my girls as they galloped past the window, giggling and screeching with mirth. And I knew that she saw her own children as they might have been and were not, and words sprang into my mind. "Rachel weeping for her children."

The baby boy hiccuped and blew milk bubbles. I held him close and again told Rachel what a fine-looking child he was. Shifting her gaze away from the window, she looked pleased with the praise. We went on to talk of the weather, about vegetables, cows and the solid wooden furniture that her husband had made for the kitchen. But we did not talk about Emberlee and Elineke – my girls. They were a visible reminder to her of the past and I was almost sorry that I had come. Every time their laughter rang through the walls, a small knife turned within her. I could feel it; I could see it.

The baby burped and we smiled at one another. Anco, Amos and some other men came in. The baby's overall health and his size were discussed by the entire group. I was wearing a winter coat – a cloth coat – and suddenly began to feel rather overheated. Actually, I was starting to feel damp. Holding the baby a little bit up and away from myself, I discovered that he had wet himself right through his diapered bundle and wet myself with it. Plastic pants were not permitted by the Amish. Rachel, Amos and every one else, thought it a huge joke to see me so discomfited and, to tell the truth, I was happy to be able to afford them some laughter.

When I left, I whispered "I'm sorry" to Miriam, adding "Your girls are in heaven." She nodded, turning away quickly. And back in the car, Emberlee and Elineke were given more leeway by us than they usually were. After all, by the grace of God, they were alive.

27

Time To Leave

Now before the Feast of the Passover, when Jesus knew that His hour had come to depart out of this world to the Father, having loved His own who were in the world, He loved them to the end. John 13:1

Secular obituaries should make us aware of the brevity of life and of the tremendously awful shock people will be in for when they come face to face with the living God. In the book *How Did They Die?* by Donaldson, a number of well-known people are recorded as saying or doing something just prior to meeting Almighty God. Actress Joan Crawford, for example, a four- time divorcée who became a Christian Scientist in her old age, died of a coronary occlusion while watching a soap opera. Actor Jackie Gleason, overweight and the big, loud man in the program 'The Honeymooners', stated: "God isn't vengeful and if you've committed a sin, He's not going to send you to hell for it." Dying of cancer, he went on to quip, "If God wants another joke man, I'm ready." Mao Tse Tung, founder of the Chinese Communist Party, was afflicted with Parkinson's Disease. Some of his last words to the members of his Politburo were: "Not many live beyond seventy. I am over eighty. I should be dead already. Didn't some of you hope I should have gone already to meet Marx?"

Obituaries mean death; they mean that life, as we know it, is gone; they mean a returning of bodies to dust; and they mean spirits returning to the God who gave them life.

Death is like going on a trip – on a journey – somewhat like going from one place to another. Obituaries can reflect on that trip. They can glorify either the goodness of temporal living, or point to the inevitability of the eternal. They can make us think of either the Lazarus or the rich-man type of nature within ourselves. They can point us to the fact that what is written about us in God's book is a thousand times more important than what is written in human books.

We often traveled together, Anco and I. Our summer holidays were a highlight. The car was packed and stacked with food, fishing gear, books, the dog and lots of games. We rose early in the morning while it was still dark. Beginning with prayer, we committed our traveling to the Lord.

How wonderful these journeys were. We rejoiced in the exceeding beauty of the Canadian landscape, in the music we had brought for our CD player, in the Louis L'Amour books on tape, in our trivial pursuit rivalry, in our special conversations, and in the picnic lunches at the wayside. Always we were amazed at the goodness of the Lord in showing us the immensity of the sky above us, outlining the greatness of His love towards us; and we constantly rejoiced in His magnificent creation. Yes, how wonderful these journeys were – mostly because we were together and together we were with God.

Now Anco's gone on a journey without me – and yet not by himself. Like Jesus, the time came for him to leave this world. It was not a going-up-north trip, as we were wont to call our summer holidays, but a journey going-on-high. Anco went on high to his Father, only because Jesus had done so many years ago and had opened the way to the Father for him. Freely Jesus left this world; freely He was crucified; and freely He died and ascended to the Father. Before He breathed His last, one of the phrases Jesus called out still echoes across the centuries: "My God, My God, why have You forsaken me?" It means that Anco and I will never be forsaken, and it means that we are redeemed.

Anco and I, we were His bride. Anco knew this and believed it. Jesus, our bridegroom, before Whom we had knelt at the onset of our marriage, showed us at His death that He loved Anco and myself to the end. We were bone of His bone and flesh of His flesh all the days of our lives.

Though I weep with Jesus' arms around me at the foot of Anco's grave, I simultaneously rejoice at the opened tomb, and I long for the resurrection of the body and the life everlasting. The inscription on our common grave reads: "We know that our Redeemer liveth" and "We shall dwell in the house of the Lord forever."

John 13:1 – don't leave your earthly home without it.

28

Keeping Animals

Of the birds according to their kinds, and of the animals according to their kinds, of every creeping thing of the ground, according to its kind, two of every sort shall come in to you to keep them alive. Genesis 6:20

It had been stipulated in Anco's Chesley Veterinary Contract that when he was on call by himself, I was to answer the telephone and notify him of any messages through the two-way radio which was installed in our kitchen. That radio crackled and spat during our breakfast, lunch and dinner and I grew to dislike it heartily as an unhealthy intruder, as a visitor who overstayed its welcome. Anco was anxious to perform well in this his first job and did not want to turn the radio off – ever. Consequently, the radio became a permanent member of our family, at least for a time.

Anco wrote down a series of questions that had to be asked should someone phone. Although I had put on a super confident act saying things like: "Sure, I can handle that!" and "There's nothing to it!," there was no denying the fact that I was a trifle apprehensive. Smiling at me over his shoulder, and carrying his large, black case, Anco left one evening and I was alone with Emberlee, Elineke and the telephone. Upstairs, the two little girls were sound asleep, but not so the phone. When it rang for the first time, I stared at it for a full thirty seconds before picking it up.

"Hello."

The greeting was not difficult and I had tried to put a smile into my voice. A deep, male voice responded.

"Is this the veterinary clinic?"

"Yes, it is."

So far so good and my hand played with the telephone cord.

"I was calling about some little wieners we want to sell."

Why in the world, I thought, would anyone want to call about a special on hot-dogs.

"Yes," I acknowledged hesitantly.

"They've ruptured in their bellies and will need some surgery before we can sell them."

"Yes," I repeated again, as it slowly dawned on me that these wieners were animals, pigs probably.

"Maybe you can tell me whether or not the Doc wants them at the clinic or whether he'll come out?"

"If you give me your number, I'll have him call you back on that."

Afterwards huge relief and yes, pride, flooded through me. The first phone call had been a success and I'd made no specific blunders after all. A few 'yesses' here and there and everything was hunky dory.

The sound of crying alerted me to the fact that I had children as well as a telephone to mind. I ran up the big, curving wooden stairs to their bedroom. Both Emberlee and Elineke were wide awake. In the mid-stage of chicken pox, they were cranky and itchy. I hoped there would be no phone calls while I bathed them in some warm water and baking soda. In God's providence, there were not. Afterwards, cosily tucked back in and refreshed, they fell asleep once more. As I closed the bedroom door softly behind me, the phone did ring again. Running down the stairs like the wind, I picked up the receiver on the third ring.

"Hello, veterinary clinic."

I congratulated myself on the three word intro, even smiling into the receiver.

"Hello, I'm phoning about a horse Doc cut last week. It's all swollen now and I wonder, could he come out soon?"

"Yes," I responded, still a bit out of breath from the dash down the stairs, "his foot's all swollen, is it?"

As soon as the words were out of my mouth, I blushed, as I suddenly remembered that the term 'cut' referred to a castration.

"Yes," I babbled on, "that's too bad. I mean, it's all swollen, is it?"

There was silence on the other end.

"The vet's out right now. Could you please leave your name and address so I can give him your message when he comes in?"

Proverbs 16:18 danced in front of me. Pride, indeed, goes before destruction and a haughty spirit before a fall.

PART III:

REACHING OUT – REACHING IN

29

I Was Sick

I was naked and you clothed Me, I was sick and you visited Me, I was in prison and you came to Me.' Matthew 25:36

Last month my daughter and I drove into Listowel to visit our friend Neil. A widower, he had been moved from his old age home to the hospital. With a bone broken in his back, walking was no longer possible. In a great deal of pain, fragile in body but strong in faith, we found him longing to go home – to his eternal home. Some of his favorite verses were from the beginning of John 14 which I read to him.

"Let not your hearts be troubled. Believe in God; believe also in me. In my Father's house are many rooms. If it were not so, would I have told you that I go to prepare a place for you? And if I go and prepare a place for you, I will come again and will take you to myself, that where I am you may be also."

He asked me to keep on reading and so I did.

Neil looked very frail and had been given morphine. But when we walked into his room, he instantly recognized both Elineke and myself and called us by name. Trustfully I asked him that, if it was possible, could he say 'hi' to Anco for me when he arrived in heaven and he smiled. I also told him that soon he would know as he was known and that Alice, his wife, and a great many others would be waiting for him and cheering him on as they stood waiting on the other side of the Jordan. He smiled again. Neil always gave everyone a very warm and loving smile.

Neil died a few weeks after our visit.

Would I have been able to witness and read John 14 and speak so freely to Neil if Anco had not died? Two of Neil's children were there and listened. And the words of Jesus comforted us all.

At Neil's funeral, it was recounted by a grandson, that Opa had been troubled in soul towards the end of his hospitalization.

"Why," he had asked his grandson, "am I still here? I can't walk. I have a lot of pain. Tell me why?"

At that moment a nurse walked in with Neil's medication. She also carried a small cup with chocolate pudding to help him to swallow the pills. Obviously in a bad humor, she scowled as she approached the bed. When she reached over to give him his drugs, Neil took the nurse's hands into his own thin, blue-veined hands, and stroked them.

"You must be very busy," he said, smiling up at her, "and yet here you are taking the time to help me. You know, you are such a blessing to me. You are doing such good work and I thank you for it."

"You are my favorite patient, Neil," she replied, softened by his kindness and gentle tone, as she proceeded to help him.

After she left, Neil turned back to his grandson, "So why am I here?" he repeated.

"You just showed me, Opa," the grandson replied.

We are, most of us, very much enmeshed in the present. But death creeps up. The grave shows no favoritism in filling its cavity and folks of all nations must admit to the reality that it is appointed for all men to die. Some, like Barabbas, are given a reprieve; some, like the rich man who built his barns, erroneously suppose that they have an eternity of living left; and some are afraid and will not even walk through churchyards, as if by avoiding walking through a cemetery, they can cancel the expiry date printed on their lives.

During the time that Anco was in the intensive care unit, the stroke unit and the palliative care area, we came across a great many people who encountered death each day. They were, of course, the doctors, the nurses, the cleaning crews, the patients and the visitors in these units. The number of visitors was few. Most patients lay in their beds quite alone with only the ceiling, the wall and their medications for company. Our family's daily attendance upon Anco was the exception rather than the rule.

In the intensive care unit, all the children were allowed into Anco's room simultaneously. They constantly spoke with their father, sang with him, prayed with him and touched him. Sad to say, Anco's lucidness of mind was ignored by doctors and he was often spoken of as if he were not present. Some nurses were very kind and others seemed detached. It grew peaceful around us when we prayed and sang, the Lord blessing others in the wards through Anco's circumstances. We were moved rather abruptly from the intensive care unit to the stroke unit, however, when I refused to comply with the attending physician's suggestion to administer certain drugs.

The stroke unit, which was a small room with four beds tightly squeezed next to one another, did not permit all the children in. It only allowed two people at a time. So the children took turns. Elineke and Scott were keeping vigil with me during the third night. But in the small hours of the morning, while they were quietly sitting by the bed, holding Anco's hand as he breathed with difficulty, they were asked to leave.

"There are too many people here," a male nurse informed us as he strode in and stood at the foot of the bed, looking fixedly at them, "so you two can't stay."

Scott got to his feet from the tiny space into which he was wedged – the space between the curtains of the next bed and Anco's bed.

"Well then I'd like to speak to the head nurse," he calmly replied.

Carrying his Bible in one hand, he made his way to the nurse's station directly across from our room. There were four nurses sitting behind the desk at the station, four people who hastily donned masks as they saw Scott approaching.

"You don't have to put the masks on for me," he addressed them, "I know you've been taking them off all evening and besides that, they don't work."

Rather sheepishly, they all took their masks off and agreed with him.

"More than a hundred nurses have been let go from this hospital for refusing to wear masks," one of them retaliated, "and although we know they don't work, we want to keep our jobs. We have mortgages to pay and food to put on the table."

"I know, and I won't report you. But I'd like to speak to the head nurse," Scott replied, "about staying the night with my father-in-law."

As they were conversing, the ward nurse joined the group.

"I understand," Scott began, addressing her directly, "that you have certain rules and regulations in this ward. But I would like to suggest to you that there is a higher moral law which overrules the civil law."

All eyes were fixed on him and he continued.

"Matthew 25 tells us that at the end of time when Jesus returns, He will judge all people. And one of the criteria He will use to judge people will be whether or not they have visited the sick. I am simply asking that you allow me to follow Jesus' instruction to visit the sick – to visit my sick father-in-law."

The ward nurse walked away but a little while later she came back and informed Scott that he was allowed to stay. He hugged her and walked back to Anco's room to continue his vigil.

It was a little while later that Anco, quite awake, looked at me steadily. His eyes held mine, but after a moment looked beyond me. Then he lowered his gaze and regarded me again, before his eyes once more extended beyond me. This continued for some time.

"What is it, sweetheart?" I asked, "Do you see Jesus? Is He calling you to come home? It's all right to go to Him. That is wonderful!"

But that moment was only a precursor of the glory that was to be Anco's very soon.

30

Never Forsaking

He answered, "Have you not read that He Who created them from the beginning made them male and female, and said, 'Therefore a man shall leave his father and his mother and hold fast to his wife, and the two shall become one flesh'? So they are no longer two but one flesh. What therefore God has joined together, let not man separate. Matthew 19:4-6

When I was a teenager, seventeen or so years old, I recall very clearly the day our cat, our black male cat, padded through the yard towards the back door meowing up a storm. My mother was mystified. Whitefoot was usually quite well-behaved. Very fond of the creature, she opened the back door to let him in, to speak to him in soothing tones, to pat him on the head and to offer him some food. The cat would not, however, be pacified by her coddling. Asking to be let out once more, he loped off into the field behind our house only to return some five minutes later, caterwauling on the back porch in an even louder pitch. Shaking her head, my mother re-opened the back door. Accompanying Whitefoot this time, was a female puss who stood by his side on the welcome mat. She was heavily pregnant and obviously in need of a good meal. Soft-hearted, my mother, who was partial to cats, fed the stray outside. But that was not the end of the matter. Whitefoot insisted, by walking in and out, that he wanted his wife of sorts, to stay. When the mummy-to-be did come into the house, (for my mother was sympathetic to her plight), her male counterpart led her to the hallway closet where she proceeded to give birth to a batch of kittens. It was beautiful in a way, to see a creature take care of its partner. A little shadow of Eden perhaps, or a small foretaste of what is to come

When Anco and I moved to Chesley, Ontario, where we lived from 1974 to 1977, we were eager to meld into the small and intimate community. Sometimes Anco would stop by the house and Emberlee, Elineke and I would go along on some of his day calls. There were also the odd times when we employed a babysitter so that I could come with him for an on-the-job date, visiting some folks Anco deemed interesting to meet. So it was that on one particular Tuesday afternoon he picked me up to accompany him on his calls and I was introduced to some beautiful people.

"You'll find Charley Fisk an amazing man," Anco told me as we were driving along in the clinic's car, his black bag bouncing up and down in the backseat at every pothole, "and while I needle his dog, you can go in and meet his wife."

"Just like that?" I responded, "Without you?"

"Sure," he smiled, "she'd love the company and Charlie would be tickled that someone would look in on her."

As we drove through Chesley, Anco told me that Charley and Anna Fisk had been married about twenty-five years and that she had become ill during the second or third year of their marriage. Diagnosed with multiple sclerosis, she was, at first, capable of attending to her housekeeping. Charley had a good job at the furniture factory in Chesley and he kept on working. In the ensuing years, however, as Anna became more and more disabled, his job whittled down to part-time, and now, at this point in their lives, he stayed home full-time. He dressed Anna, fed her, put denture powder on her teeth, set them in her mouth, and read her the local newspaper as well as numerous books. When I walked into the kitchen-dining room of sorts that afternoon, he was just washing her face. The washcloth was a clean rag and Charley scrubbed hard – scrubbed hard enough, it seemed to me, to wear away her translucent skin. Yet Anna, a frail-looking woman, smiled up at him all the while he was washing her. Probably because he was beaming down at her as well. Laundry hung everywhere from lines strung up between the rafters. I had to bend over not to disturb towels and linens as I walked over to shake hands. Anna sat in a black, leather wheelchair. Her hands were thin and white and rested in her lap. I took one of the limp hands into my own and said, "How do you do," and "Pleased to meet you." Then I shook Charley's hands. His was a firm grip which almost crushed my own into pulp.

"So glad you stopped by," Charley said, "Shall I make you a cup of tea?"

Anco, who was just walking in at this point, shook his head.

"No, thanks, Charley. We have to get going again. I just thought I'd bring my wife in to meet you."

Both of them smiled at me. I smiled back. There were numerous bowls of cat food on the floor, and several cats lounged about on the window sill and on the hospital bed by the window. Charley saw me glance at the hospital bed and explained.

"That's where Anna sleeps," he began, and then pointing over to an old couch across from it, he continued, "and that's where I sleep so I can keep an eye on her."

He winked at me and I blushed. He laughed.

"The truth is," he went on, "that this way we can see one another at night."

One form for the solemnization of marriage reads:

> Marriage, then, is a divine ordinance intended to be a source of happiness to man, an institution of the highest significance to the human race, and a symbol of the union of Christ and His Church. We may, therefore, as Christians look with confidence for grace in the discharge of our mutual responsibilities and for guidance and help in our common perplexities and trials (Form for the Solemnization of Marriage of the Christian Reformed Church (1912)).

That same marriage formulary goes on to admonish the bridegroom: "... do you promise that you will, with the gracious help of God, love, honor and maintain her, live with her in the holy bonds of marriage according to God's ordinance, and never forsake her, so long as you both shall live."

Charley obviously and cheerfully kept that promise to God. I do not recall much else about Charley and Anna Fisk. But I do know that they were examples to Anco and me – examples of the commitment and self-sacrifice which Jesus calls us to have for one another. For He said to all of us: A new commandment I give to you, that you love one another: just as I have loved you, you also are to love one another.

31

Providence

The Lord has made everything for its purpose, even the wicked for the day of trouble. Proverbs 16:4

The intimacies and implications of Lord's Day 10 were not imprinted on my pea-size brain yet when I was a child. Olevianus and Ursinus were, during my early school and skinned-knees days, complete strangers to me. It was only later that I began to see that, as it is phrased in Lord's Day 10:

> God's providence is His Almighty and ever-present power, whereby, as with His hand, He still upholds heaven and earth and all creatures, and so governs them that leaf and blade, rain and drought, fruitful and barren years, food and drink, health and sickness, riches and poverty, indeed, all things, come to us not by chance but by His Fatherly hand (Heidelberg Catechism, Q&A 27).

For a long time I had the mistaken notion that hardships, (and everyone has them), somehow took away God-given opportunities. Gradually, through the generous outpouring of the Holy Spirit's renewal in my heart, I came to know better. Indeed, I began to understand that Proverbs 16:4 and Lord's Day 10 shook hands and graciously invited me to agree with them.

Even so, there are the days when I look back and reflect on whether or not I could, or should have done, anything that would have prevented Anco's stroke. At those times I stumble in my faith. Questions begin to jump up and down in my mind and heart like a child on a trampoline. Had I been aware enough of his difficulties, of the things he could not do any longer? Was his diet sufficient or should I have added something to it? Was he feeling unwell and did this pass by me unnoticed?

It's easy to become lost in self-reproach; to think an action could have altered the time and outcome of the glory that God inevitably had in mind. Because, in the long run, the number of days which God has meted out to each one of us are exactly so many – not one more or one less than He has decided.

There was also an exact time when our Lord Jesus was crucified and there was a very specific hour for His death. He was the Passover Lamb without blemish and He was slain on the fourteenth day of Nisan. Sacrificed for us, He died at three p.m., the same hour that the paschal lambs were being slain.

At the particular time of Jesus' death, many people were visiting Jerusalem to go up to the Passover feast. To get into the city, these visitors passed Golgotha, consequently seeing the inscription on His cross which read: "Jesus of Nazareth, the King of the Jews." God meant for these visitors to be in Jerusalem to witness this sign on this precise day.

Even so God, Who controls all thing for His purposes, had a purpose in the exact time and place of Anco's death. In the intensive care unit, in the stroke unit and in the palliative care unit, we sang, read Scripture and prayed. A great many people in the rooms and beds around Anco, heard the gospel proclaimed. We were in effect an inscription which read: "Jesus of Nazareth, the King of Kings, died, rose, and ascended into heaven."

Jesus knew that He would die. He knew how and He knew when and He continually spoke of His hour!

We, on the other hand, have no such foreknowledge. The fact that Jesus knew when He would die and how He would die, added to His agony. The fact that we do not know when or how we will die, can be said to be a blessing. And because Jesus chose wittingly and wilfully to be the Lamb, we need never be afraid of the way or time of our death.

Left to myself, I might have chosen some other time and consequently would have missed what glory God had in mind with the hour of Anco's death. What lofty concepts both the providence of God and His foreknowledge are! These concepts eventually throw me down to the ground, down to my knees. Nothing occurs without the Father's love. Nothing occurs without the Father's will. For I was chosen in Him before the foundation of the world to be holy and blameless in His sight; and He predestined Anco to be adopted as His son, and me to be adopted as His daughter.

32

Animals

It is I who by My great power and My outstretched arm have made the earth, with the men and animals that are on the earth, and I give it to whomever it seems right to Me. Jeremiah 27:5

The Farenhorst in-laws were over for a visit and because they absolutely relished the idea of staying with their grandchildren, I was able to visit the clinic with Anco that particular Saturday night of their stay.

Anco told me on the way to the clinic that it was a porcupine call and that a dog would be coming in with quills all over his body. I visualised huge quills sticking out of a dog's nose and ears, and conjured up pictures of Anco extracting them with precision and skill, blood spattering onto his immaculate, white coat. However, when the dog, a big brown and white mutt, was carried into the surgery by the owner, a man who was accompanied and flanked by two grown sons, I could see no quills at all.

The patient was obviously not feeling very well. Placed on the operating table, he sat subdued and blinked nervously.

"All right," Anco instructed, anaesthetic needle poised in his hand, "now be sure you fellows hold on to him well because this will sting just a bit."

Anco, I'm sure, was recalling the last dog he'd needled, a dog who had turned and bit him rather fiercely. Fortunately, it had been an old mongrel without any teeth. The present dog with the quills whimpered miserably and one of the boys obligingly moved next to the table, clasping his pet in a hug of sorts. The needle sank in and, after about five minutes, the dog perceptibly became sleepy. During the waiting time, one of the boys told us that the canine was a Heinz breed, a mixture of many things. Anco divulged that he liked that variety the best. As the beast slowly sank sideways towards the rather stern-faced owner who had taken his son's place next to the table, he was caught and laid down.

"Go to seep, now," the strapping fellow whispered in a simulated baby voice, and I had trouble not to grin, "Go to seep, doggy."

Anco had fetched a bowl of water, and a pair of forceps. He now began checking the front paws for quills. Tiny pin points, barely visible, protruded from the fur. Anco would take hold of one and pull it back and forth, back and forth – and out it came. The quills were little, with tiny, fish hook barbs at their ends. These barbs enabled the quills to travel throughout the dog and come out anywhere from eye to brain.

"I've taken out about thirty or so myself at home," the owner informed us, "Couldn't get all of them though."

"I see some scratches around the scrotum," Anco said, by way of response, "Did you extract any there?"

"No! No!" was the immediate answer, "Those scratches are probably the result of the flea collar he was wearing."

Funny place to have a flea collar, I thought. Then I realized that the man did not know what scrotum meant and I blushed for him. Anco kept quiet and I was glad that he did not catch my eye for I would have giggled. He just went on working, pulling and yanking quills out of the dog's gums and tongue. It did not look very pleasant so I turned away to stand by the window.

"Well, that's about it," Anco eventually told the family of onlookers, "He'll be out for a couple of hours and before you go home, I'll give him a shot of long-lasting penicillin to see him through the next few days. There shouldn't be any problems though."

"Great, Doc. Thanks very much."

Back home the girls were still up with Opa and Oma Farenhorst. Before being bundled off to bed, they sang a chorus of "Jesus bids me shine with a pure, pure light. Like a little candy, shining in the night." Opa Farenhorst especially relished the girls' heartfelt rendition of the song.

God did not give us eyes to see whether or not sad days lay ahead. It would only be a year and a half before Opa Farenhorst, our dear father and father-in-law, would see his Savior face to face. The years of his life would number three score and two. Spurgeon, that dear preacher, said it well when he reflected:

> Dark days may be near at hand for some of us, but we do not perceive them. Let us be thankful that we do not, for our afflictions would be multiplied at the foresight of them. The prospect of evil to come might cast a gloom over pleasure near at hand. As we may feel a thousand deaths in fearing one, so we may faint under a single stroke in dreading a thousand.

33

My Rock and My Refuge

Hear my cry, O God, listen to my prayer; from the end of the earth I call to you when my heart is faint. Lead me to the rock that is higher than I, for You have been my refuge, a strong tower against the enemy. Psalm 61:1-3

Sometimes when I'm sad, I feel sluggish, and things tend to overwhelm me. Things happen too swiftly and my mind cannot comprehend or fasten onto one thing or another. At that time I need to seek a quiet place and go on my knees and just lean against the Lord. He is always there, as solid as a rock because He is the Rock.

The letters keep on coming. Every day when I walk to the mailbox by the road, the dog trotting by my side, the little red flag is up. 'Letters here', it whispers. There are bills, advertisements and cards. The thing is that the cards, and this is a new thing and difficult to comprehend, are all addressed to me. "Dear Christine," and "Dearest Christine," they say. It is like getting a new name. My name used to be "Anco and Christine." I am cut off at the beginning. It seems I am alone – an orphan, as it were.

But then I remember the comfort Jesus gave when He left the disciples. They had also always been closely connected to a name – His name. It was constantly "Jesus and the disciples." Frequently associated in His address, they seemed to be one with Him.

Before Jesus left the earth, He deeply sensed their upcoming loneliness and He wanted to assure them that their personal relationship, their union to Him, would only grow stronger. So He told them a Counselor would come to them. He told them they would know this Counselor because He would live in them. Jesus stressed that He would not leave them as orphans but would come to them.

Dwelling on that, on my knees, I hear Jesus say to me: "I went away to die for you. And I live in you now."

I know this truth very deeply within myself and know also that Anco and I have always been, and always will be, part of a multitude. We were, and are, Christ's sheep. We were, and are, God's chosen. We can never be unattached. We were, and are, and forever will be, part of Jesus.

And a voice within me whispers, "You are not alone."

34

Blessings

Blessed be the God and Father of our Lord Jesus Christ, Who has blessed us in Christ with every spiritual blessing in the heavenly places. Ephesians 1:3

One evening in the fall of 1975, we took Anco's Dad and Mom out to dinner to tell them that a third little Farenhorst was on the way. They were overjoyed, as were we. Later that same night, Dad Farenhorst experienced severe chest pain, was rushed to the hospital and, subsequently, was diagnosed with lung cancer.

Sir James Barrie, the author of *Peter Pan,* when he was an old man, refused to make appointments, even social ones, if he thought the date was too distant down the weeks. "I'm an old man," he said, "short notice now." The brevity and certainly the uncertainty of life, should be enough to make all of us stop and think about what road it is on which we travel and whether today might be the last stretch we will be allowed to travel. You can't plan for death, or can you?

1975-76 was a difficult and traumatic year. We often drove to Hamilton on weekends to be with Dad Farenhorst. He very much enjoyed seeing his little granddaughters, Emberlee and Elineke. They crawled into his bed and regaled him with stories. As he became weaker and weaker, his desire for heaven grew stronger and stronger.

"It is as if I see a door," he told us, "and it is open just a crack. But week by week the door opens wider and I see light shining through."

Tante Til, Opa Farenhorst's sister, came over from Holland. We paid for her plane ticket ostensibly so that she could help me after the baby was born, but the truth was that we hoped she would still be able to see her brother.

Tante Til was cheerful, full of common sense, laughter and love. In April of 1976 our son Christopher Dirk was born, two days after Tante Til's arrival. We named him Christopher, signifying 'Christ-bearer' and his second name, Dirk, was chosen in honor of his paternal Opa, Dirk Farenhorst.

Unfortunately, the day I went into labor, Tante Til was down with the flu and unable to leave her bed. Anco, in the early hours of that Monday morning, had to bring the two girls to a friend's house even as I helped Tante Til sit up in bed, furnishing her with a pail in case she had to throw up.

"Och, kindje! Och, kindje!" (something akin to 'You poor child! You poor child!), was a phrase she kept repeating, and "You are in labor?!! Oh!! Oh!!!"

It did not matter that I kept assuring her that I was fine, even though every now and then my breathing became rather unsteady. She was devastated.

When Anco came home, an hour or so later, things seemed well under control. I had cleaned, fed and encouraged Tante Til who, at this point, looked chipper. After hugging her goodbye, Anco and I left, stopping at the post office to pick up our mail before driving on to the Hanover Hospital. It was late morning by this time. I was checked into the Hanover 'Hilton', as it was known, given the Frisian enema, and brought into a labor room. Anco appeared shortly thereafter with our favorite labor book – the Jewish one by Leo Rosten. He read me several pages and we would laugh, except when I was doing heavy breathing. Nurses came to listen and laugh alongside our bed and around 4:30 it was deemed time by the attending nurse to call in the doctor who was on duty. The doctor, a proud South African, loved the fact that we were Dutch. He continually repeated the South African phrase "Alles sal reg kom. Alles sal reg kom." Translated that phrase means "Everything will be all right." When Christopher's head emerged, he enthusiastically called out, "It's a boy!" Anco immediately told me that he could not possibly know if this was true, but the next push confirmed the doctor's prognosis.

That night I was awakened by the nurse around 2:00 a.m. It was not to feed little Christopher, but to hear her tell me that she had never before seen a child smile so sweetly at less than half a day old.

Christopher – Christ-bearer – was a covenant child. Anco and I were privileged in that God permitted us to train him and to pray every day that the Holy Spirit would dwell in him. It was a planning for his death.

God has been pleased to answer our training and our prayers. Christopher Dirk is now in his forties and the father of eight children of his own. He is preparing his children for death as well. Grandfather Farenhorst, who also planned his death and for whom Christopher was named, has been with Jesus almost half a century.

Most people plan. They plan to get up out of bed in the morning; they plan to have breakfast; they plan to work, to relax and to go to bed again at night. We are a generation of those who look ahead, even handing out daily planners to students. To a certain degree that is good. We can't live without a certain amount of scheduling. But then there is death – that untimely, inconvenient and intrusive enemy – death! Depicted as the Grim Reaper, an unsightly skeleton walking about with a scythe, he is unwelcome and never desirable to the ordinary citizen walking about the street simply minding his own business.

You can't plan for death. Or can you?

35

Treasures

My soul will be satisfied as with fat and rich food, and my mouth will praise You with joyful lips, when I remember You upon my bed, and meditate on You in the watches of the night; for You have been my help, and in the shadow of Your wings I will sing for joy. Psalm 63:5-7

Every day I remember many things about Anco: what he said, did, wrote, and how he laughed and cried. These last years he was active in prison ministry and wrote to some men in prison, helping them with Bible study. Prior to doing that, he penned the following words:

> We do not know in whose heart the Lord will work, but we do know that one of the principal means He uses is through the interaction of believers with others. I believe God may be able to use me with my limited abilities to be a blessing to others by this means.
>
> A question to ask may be 'What is there that God has not done for me?' I Corinthians 4:7 says: 'For what do you have that you did not receive?' I owe my life to my gracious Saviour. In thankfulness to Him I am trying to live my life in dedication to Him as much as I am able.

In 1968, just prior to our engagement in the fall of that year, I traveled to Tallahassee, Florida, to help my sister, Johanna, who was expecting her third baby. It was my first trip on an airplane, and Anco, my Dad and my Mom, brought me to the then-named Toronto Malton airport. Anco began writing me a letter to read on the plane as we were sitting in the airport waiting room, anticipating my boarding call.

> My dearest Sweetheart, By the time you read this, which is right now for you, you will be in the plane or in Tallahassee. How does it feel, sweetheart? Lonesome? Happy? I feel lonely now already and you're sitting right across the room from me. We are all talking, your Dad, Mom, you and me, and your Dad's looking at the plane ticket.
>
> Boy, sweetheart, this is going to be quite something, but time goes pretty fast and before you know it, we'll all be back at Malton – only this time leaving for Fruitland. I wonder how you'll find Florida? You know I don't think you'll find it much different from here. Maybe the people will act a little different though. I have the feeling they'll be stiffer, more reserved there, but this is only speculation.

Always enamored by the north, he ended his letter with a little poem. It certainly made me smile as I read it, and I loved it. I still do.

> If I was at the South Pole and you were at the North,
> I'd be a little penguin soul, and you would sally forth,
> Clad out in all your seal skins, and on your hands more fur,
> Would you, dear, cross the distance, to say 'I do' and brrr.

He was quite proud of this piece of literature. He ended his efforts by saying:

> PS I love you
> PPS I love you more
> PPPS I love you still more

Sometimes when a day has gone particularly badly, and I miss Anco very, very much, I permit myself the luxury of reading one of his letters from long ago before I go to sleep. They are comforting, and I am so thankful for them. They are God's gifts to me.

However, I would be much remiss to say that Anco's letters are the only or best comforts I have. Every evening before I go to sleep, and every morning when I awake, as well as during the day, I am able to read words from my heavenly Bridegroom, words which are readily available on my night table and by the living room table.

I may, and must, read the Bible, as J.C. Ryle said, like someone digging for buried treasure.

36

Bringing Good News

Whoever brings blessing will be enriched, and one who waters will himself be watered. Proverbs 11:25

Tante Til was a blessing to us during her Chesley stay. She had an admirable sense of cleanliness and believed in utilizing items properly. She wouldn't dream of having a soup bowl function as a cat dish or using a handkerchief to wipe a cobweb (the latter sin of which Anco was often guilty). Tante Til was not overly fond of cats and our kitten, having been dubbed 'Little Grape' by the girls, had to stay out of her way. The litter box was *'vies'* or 'dirty' and she wouldn't touch it. So Anco had to clean it while I was in the hospital. He did so, with our silver salad fork. We had never found much use for this wedding present, and it served admirably in the capacity of litter box utensil. We had somehow failed to inform Tante Til of this rather disreputable habit. The large fork lay against the wall on the kitchen counter, ready for use whenever called upon. It was a dirty black because I had an intense aversion to cleaning silverware.

One of my first nights home from the hospital, Tante Til cooked a special supper – mashed potatoes, vegetables, pork chops, applesauce and salad. It looked scrumptious. As we sat down and tied bibs around the girls' necks, Tante Til shone with goodwill.

"Nou, eet maar lekker, jongens." "Eat hearty, guys."

We prayed and then began to put food on our plates. It was not until Anco began scooping some lettuce onto his plate, that he suddenly noticed that he was holding the silver litter fork. Only the fork was not ladling out litter but green salad. His second scoop, therefore, hung in mid-air. He caught my eye and there was a helpless expression on his face. I grinned at him, only he didn't grin back.

"Good salad, isn't it, sweetheart?" I said.

"Dank je." "Thank you."

Tante Til beamed from her end of the table, *"Zal ik jou ook wat geven?"* "Shall I give you some too?"

"No, thank you," I answered virtuously, "it might spoil the baby's milk."

Anco ate around the salad even as Tante Til explained in detail how she had polished the fork which she had found on the counter and wasn't it nice and shiny now? Then she gently admonished me to take better care of the silverware.

We later brought Tante Til to Hamilton and she spent many days with her brother. They reminisced, laughed and prayed together. She was a blessing to him and to other members of the family.

Tante Til not only had a wonderful sense of laughter and love, but also delighted in narrating a story about her father, Anco's grandfather. She, (as well as her sister, Tante To), must have recounted that story to us three or four times on different occasions.

"Every time there was a thunderstorm at night," she would begin, "and I was afraid, my father would open the curtains of my bedroom window and point to the lightning streaking across the sky. I would huddle under the blankets, so terrified that I would be close to tears. Then he would say, 'God is the one Who scatters the lightning. The thunder is His voice. Little girl, do you not have a mighty God? And He is your Father and He loves you.' Then my father would sit on the edge of my bed and I would not be afraid anymore."

How wonderful to have relatives who recount the might of God!

37

Known

For now we see in a mirror dimly, but then face to face. Now I know in part; then I shall know fully, even as I have been fully known. 1 Corinthians 13:12

Every now and then it is as if I suddenly wake up and discern for the first time that Anco is not with me any longer. These are the times such as before breakfast when I reach for his hand in prayer; or the moment I come home from shopping, eager to see how he is, eager to tell him what I've bought; or the instant I open the car door on the passenger side and realize that I am the driver now; or the second I roll over in bed in order to feel the warmth of his back and his legs; and the occasion I glance out the window to catch sight of him walking across the driveway to the car bay. All these things occur abruptly, out of the blue, and they happen all the time. And my stomach lurches each time, and I know for a fact that it is true. Anco will not come to me, but I will go to him.

One of my daughters has told me that I did not prepare her enough for the pain of childbirth, that I only intimated that it was very hard work. Perhaps then, I ponder, I should prepare my children for this pain of death. For, oh, I do acknowledge that this pain of death is much, much worse than the momentary affliction of bearing a child. For, after all, at the end of labor you hold a child and all pain is forgotten.

But then this truth pursues me. The truth that I will see a face after this intense pain and I will know this face. It will be the face of my Savior, my Redeemer. And I will know as

I am known. Anco already knows and the truth is that his pain is gone forever. I now see Anco look at me from fading photographs and I perceive him smiling at me from fleeting events that have withered like grass. But later ....

My husband had a heart for the gospel and for evangelization.

When he was a young boy, around eleven or twelve years old, Anco often played road hockey on the street with friends. During one game, the ball they were using as puck dropped down into a sewer hole. Anco held up the sewer lid while his brother recovered the ball. Then, after the ball had been fished out, he inadvertently dropped the lid on his foot. His right, big toe was almost severed under the weight of the heavy lid. Although, amazingly, Anco managed to shuffle home slowly, his Dad had to take him to the hospital where he remained for a few weeks. A skin graft from his thigh was required to reshape the right toe. Anco consequently had a rather misformed, right big toe. Yet, in the eyes of God, Anco's feet were beautiful! Maturing into a godly man, he brought good news to fellow workers, neighbors and acquaintances; he always recounted the might of God; he spoke of peace; and he consistently told his children, and grandchildren, that God reigned supreme.

Anco was fully known by God and now sees Him face to face. He knew in part but now knows fully.

The day will come when he will look at me again with abiding love and I can hardly wait for both of us to worship our Lord and Savior fully and eternally.

38

Days of Light and Darkness

Light is sweet, and it is pleasant for the eyes to see the sun. So if a person lives many years, let him rejoice in them all; but let him remember that the days of darkness will be many. All that comes is vanity. Ecclesiastes 11:7-8

The seventies were a busy decade, because five little Farenhorsts were born into them. It was a sad decade as well, as our dear father and Opa, Dick Farenhorst died of cancer. A month or two prior to his death, he was still able to hold his first grandson, Christopher, in his arms. But, weak as he was, he could only hold him for a moment.

Editor of *Calvinist Contact*, a Dutch/Canadian Christian weekly, from 1959 to 1976, Dick Farenhorst loved the Lord with all his heart and was a godly influence to the post-war influx of immigrants from Holland in both his writing and his walk of life. It was still dark outside the early morning hour that the telephone call came informing us that Dad had gone to be with the Lord. This was the first time I saw Anco sob uncontrollably. After he hung up the receiver, he sat down on the edge of the bed. Then his shoulders began to heave and he turned to me for comfort. We cried, prayed and clung to one another for a long time, but not as those who have no hope.

During the summer of 1977, two important events happened. The first one was that Anco accepted a job at the veterinary clinic in Owen Sound. There were already two vets in this busy practice and he became a welcome third. We were hoping and praying for a less hectic pace of life, for more time together with the family. In conjunction with this job change, we moved from Chesley to Owen Sound and bought our first house. The house we purchased was a little, yellow, brick bungalow. Hesitatingly, we dared call it our own, ignoring the specter of the hefty mortgage dangling from its reddish roof. It had a walkout basement, three bedrooms and, best of all, a lovely neighbor who would prove to be a surrogate grandmother to our children.

The second important event that summer was that we were given our fourth child. I went into labor on August 1, a Monday. Anco came home from his calls in the early evening and brought Emberlee, Elineke and Christopher to some friends. Coming back home, impressed by the quiet and peace, he became somewhat sentimental and rather romantic.

We sat together on the couch, with me huffing and puffing every ten minutes and Anco relaxing and smiling at me, even saying: "Wish we could do this more often. It's so nice being alone together."

It was not something to which I could readily relate in those moments. Around 10:00, I suggested that it was probably time to leave for the hospital.

"Oh, sweetheart," he responded with a huge smile, "are you sure? Maybe we could still watch a movie or something? Just for a little while?"

I was adamant, however, that it was time to leave. I had trouble getting into the car and arriving at the hospital, Anco had to manoeuver me from the front seat into a wheelchair. At breakneck speed, he pushed me to the mainfloor elevator, at which point a nurse took over as he left to park the car.

"Your fourth baby?" she inquired, even as I inhaled and exhaled heavily, "Oh, my, we'd better hurry."

Our doctor was on holidays. After the nurses prepped me, I was wheeled straight into delivery. The attending physician, an older gentleman by the name of Dr. McConachie, marched into the room and took charge. Although he was a little rough around the edges, he knew exactly what he was doing. Anco had made it to the delivery room as well, and stood by my side, encouraging me faithfully.

"That's it, sweetheart. You're doing fine."

It was close to midnight. A few pushes and there she was, our beautiful, dark-haired little angel.

"Nothing wrong with this kid!" Dr. McConachie boomed out as he whumped her on her tiny, little butt.

Charity Larissa emitted a long wail before she was put onto my tummy. She was so bonnie. It was just after midnight – August 2.

My Dad and Mom arrived at the hospital first thing the next morning. Because they had not come during the mandated visiting hours, they were not allowed into my room and I had to walk over to the waiting area to see them. My Dad, never shy, prayed a wonderfully long and loud prayer which exalted God and praised Him for His covenant goodness. Later one of the nurses came in to see me. She was a black woman and a kind nurse.

"Your father's prayer really moved me," she told me, "I did so appreciate his words. There are not many families like yours around."

Anco's pet name for Charity was 'little punkie'. I don't know why. Emberlee, Elineke and Christopher were not allowed into the hospital to see their new baby sister. So Anco huddled them together into a small group on the hospital parking lot. He had alerted me as to when to stand in front of the hospital's second story window, where I waved and blew kisses at my excited brood.

It is good to remember on a daily basis that God is visible in the heavens and that by looking up we can be heartened by His might and beauty. The truth is that we can literally see Him bestowing His love and care as we gaze up at the window pane of the sky. Isaiah 40 nudges us to stand like children in the parking lot of our earthly existence. Indeed, that fine prophet nudges us to dance in amazement and happiness, as we behold what the Lord Jesus has created.

To whom then will you compare Me, that I should be like him? says the Holy One. Lift up your eyes on high and see Who created these? He Who brings out their host by number, calling them all by name; by the greatness of His might and because He is strong in power, not one is missing.

39

Sharing Comfort

Praise be to the God and Father of our Lord Jesus Christ, the Father of compassion and the God of all comfort, Who comforts us in all our troubles, so that we can comfort those in any trouble with the comfort we ourselves receive from God. 2 Corinthians 1:3-4

It has been on my mind recently that what I presently need in my bereavement is not what I myself have always given to those who were bereaved.

We had been married almost eight years when we moved into that first home in Owen Sound in 1977. The little, brick bungalow boasted a bit of yellow siding. It was tiny, to be sure, but it was ours. Three small bedrooms, plus the possibility of a fourth in the basement, as well as a nice backyard bordering a farmer's field, made us feel quite the landowners.

We were much closer to church than we had been in Chesley, and two doors down we acquired Christian neighbors. I was expecting our Charity at that point and had my hands splendidly full with a four, three and one year old. The neighbors, Opa and Oma V, proved to be grand! Opa had dementia and although I heard rumors that he had been a feisty man when younger, he was tenderhearted at this point of his life and spent many hours playing games with Elineke.

One morning, that first summer in Owen Sound, the phone rang. It was Oma V's daughter-in-law.

"Can you please go and check on Dad and Mom. Mom just phoned and something's wrong with Dad."

I ran over and found Mrs. V distraught. She took me to the bathroom where her husband was lying in the bathtub – naked with a little washcloth discreetly covering his privates.

"I think he's had a heart attack," she whispered, "but I don't know if he's dead!"

Elineke was in the livingroom and Emberlee, almost five, was minding Christopher. Together Mrs. V and I held a mirror up to Opa's mouth. Much to our relief, it showed a small cloud of breath. An ambulance was on the way and so was Anco, who arrived shortly after I did. Anco drove with Oma in the ambulance to the hospital. Opa V died a few days later.

Oma V was a godly lady. For years afterwards she helped me with everything. She sewed, cooked and babysat. She was magnificent!

During this time I became like a daughter to her. We visited people together, went to Bible study together and when my back gave out, she came for days on end to cook and clean. A remarkable widow who loved God, she told me that when I had moved two doors down just prior to her 'Hendrik's' death, that I had been God's gift to her.

There was one occasion when I picked Oma up for Bible study. Walking over to the car, she gave me a huge grin. I immediately noticed with some consternation that she had forgotten to put her teeth in. Beginning to speak, I hesitated, became nervous and swallowed my words. Perhaps, I conjectured, there were days when she went without them. As the car slowly backed out of the driveway, Oma V comfortably settled in next to me. Smoothing out her skirt, she commented that the weather was beautiful. I nodded but was worried, trying hard to think of how I should broach the subject of her teeth. Would the ladies in the Bible study make fun of her? Turning onto the road and beginning to drive towards the church, I frantically picked my brain to come up with a natural way to bring up the missing dentures. It was at least five minutes into driving when she suddenly burst out in Dutch: "*K'heb mien tanden vergeten! Och, waarom heb ie niks ezegt.*" (I forgot my teeth! Oh, why didn't you say anything!")

I grinned, turned the car around and we drove back to pick up her teeth.

There is something more affecting. I cannot remember initially speaking to Oma V of her loss – the loss of her dear husband. Later we spoke of him frequently, but not after he first passed. It is something I now know I should have done in those first few months. She must have grieved much and I could have been a shoulder on which to weep.

I received a card in the mail today from a friend who lost her husband a number of years ago. It read:

> Dear Christine: Just a short note to say I think of you and pray for you often. We will continue to miss our dear husbands but will be also reminded of them in good ways – as we go about our activities and family visits. Keep his memory alive! This life is short and the Lord still has work for us to do – Praise God! Delight in Him, do His good work and one day may we also be before the Lord hearing those wonderful words,
>
> 'Well done, thou good and faithful servant, enter into My rest.' It is O.K. to feel down at times because we miss our husbands .... I am so thankful for the many fruits of our union and the fact that our 'heavenly Husband' is always ready to listen and help us with anything. Praise God from Whom all blessings flow.

This friend understands that one of the reasons we are given hardships by God, "is ... so that we may be able to comfort those who are in any affliction, with the comfort with which we ourselves are comforted by God" (2 Cor. 1:4b).

40

Praying and Singing

The memory of the righteous is a blessing. Proverbs 10:7a

This morning after I took care of the chickens and had breakfast, I began to sort things out in the basement. Building the sunroom has created a mess of many items which were stored in haphazard fashion. The utility room has closet space, so I began folding up blankets and pillows, laying them down on the shelves in neat order. But every blanket was precious in my hands and every pillow made me see Anco's face. My sorting out did not last all that long. My crying did.

We prayed – each of us kneeling down at our own side of the bed, hands folded on the blanket. We did this each evening. In the morning, we knelt in the bed itself – each with a face scrunched down into our own pillow. After Anco had his first stroke we just prayed while sitting up in bed, with him holding my hands. Why does the memory of such a good thing make me so incredibly sad?

Psalm 95:1 says: "Oh come, let us sing to the LORD; let us make a joyful noise to the rock of our salvation!" Psalm 95:1 was our bedfellow. He was between us, next to us and behind us. And He is still there next to and behind me now.

When the kids were little, we often sang with them around the supper table. We sang with them around the piano each Sunday evening. Considering singing together a joy, we introduced our progeny to Psalm 95:1 at an early age, praying that verse 6, (Oh come, let us worship and bow down; let us kneel before the LORD, our Maker!), would become an intimate friend.

Singing is one preparation for heaven, said the Quaker, John Bevan. Anco deeply loved singing. He sang psalms and hymns with gusto. He sang in the bathtub, in the car, while he was woodworking, and, of course, in church. After his first stroke, his voice became a lot weaker and this rendered him increasingly frustrated and sad. In heaven, he hoped to be able to play the violin like Itzhak Perlman and sing like Pavarotti. I don't know if either of these gentlemen will be in heaven, but I know that my Anco will be.

41

Children Yet Unborn

He established a testimony in Jacob and appointed a law in Israel, which He commanded our fathers to teach to their children, that the next generation might know them, the children yet unborn, and arise and tell them to their children, so that they should set their hope in God and not forget the works of God, but keep his commandments. Psalm 78:5-7

The summer of 1978 was a busy summer, but a good summer. Our newly dug out vegetable patch seemed to be thriving and the older children ran in and around the house like little puppies, happy to be alive and flourishing. On hot days I attached the sprinkler to the garden hose. It turned wildly as Emberlee, Elineke and Christopher whooped and galloped through the droplets. One afternoon, as I was watching them out of the corner of my eye from the kitchen window during supper preparations, the phone rang. It was Sharon, an acquaintance, who had moved from Owen Sound to London, Ontario a few years before. After niceties had been exchanged, she came directly to the point.

"Christine, I'm phoning to ask if you and Anco could do me a favor?"

"If we can," I answered, "we surely will. What is it?"

"My second daughter," she said, "is expecting a baby and I wonder if she can come and live with you for a while?"

"Expecting?" I repeated, "And her husband ...?"

"She's not married," Sharon's voice shook but then continued, "She's only a teenager, and she wants to have an abortion."

"Oh," I murmured, and felt my own baby stir within my belly.

We were expecting our fifth child and he was a mover.

"People are so unforgiving," Sharon went on, "and it would be good for her to live in an area where no one knows her after she has the abortion."

"Oh, Sharon," I cried, "I can't believe you want her to have an abortion."

There was a long silence before she said, "No, I don't. But I don't know how to stop her."

Anco and I spoke together that evening. We decided that we would welcome the girl into our home with open arms. She could live with us, eat with us, sleep with us, and worship with us. We were prepared to love her and to help her in any way we could. But the proviso to taking her in would be dependent upon her not getting an abortion. We agreed that I would drive to London to have a talk with the girl.

The upshot of the matter was that a few days later I drove to London and had a long conversation, first with mother Sharon and later with her daughter. I prayed with the girl, offering her our love, our home, our care and our acceptance. Almost at the point of coming back to Owen Sound with me that very day, she backed out at the last minute. I left our phone number in case she changed her mind, but she never called. Anco and I were never privy to what eventually happened.

From time-to-time God placed matters of vital importance on our path, and choices had to be made that fell in line with His Word. There were occasions which left us clueless as to the final outcome of a decision, but we were never ignorant as to the direct imperatives of God's commandments.

Spurgeon said: "We are not responsible to God for the souls that are saved, but we are responsible for the Gospel that is preached, and for the way in which we preach it"

42

Jewelry

On that day, declares the LORD of hosts, I will take you, O Zerubbabel My servant, the son of Shealtiel, declares the LORD, and make you like a signet ring, for I have chosen you, declares the LORD of hosts." Haggai 2:23

February 4, 1966 was always a special day for Anco and me. On that day Anco had gifted me with a ring. It was a Friday and we took a city bus to a little downtown Hamilton store called 'The Jewel Box'. Anco had actually already given me a little ring that previous Christmas. It had been carefully tucked away under the cap of a perfume bottle. When he presented me with the perfume, waiting anxiously for me to open the bottle and to smell its scent, the little piece of jewelry underneath the cap immediately became evident. The ring actually looked a little like something you get out of a bubble gum machine, but I loved it. Anco, however, wanted very much to give me something a little more lasting and hence the trip to 'The Jewel Box'. He showed me a beautiful gold band with two small, pink gemstones perched on top. I loved it and he had the words 'Love is eternal' engraved inside the band. Both rings were very special to me. Wearing something which Anco had given me put, as it were, a mark on me which said: "I belong to this man." He bought it for me with his hard-earned money to demonstrate that he loved me and that I was a part of him.

Anco and his family all came to the Fruitland church the Sunday I made my profession of faith in the spring of 1966.

It was a few months after the purchase of the ring. It was one of the few times in my life that I wore a hat, a blue, little thing, which my mother and I had bought together. She also bought me a blue skirt and matching top. But those vestments, although nice, were truly of very little account.

Matthew 6:33 was the text my father bestowed on me, the text he read out loud after I said 'I do' as I stood in the pew along with a dozen or so other young people. At that precise moment I felt as if I was standing before the very throne of God and was verbally committing my life to Him. The text my father gave me was akin to a beautiful necklace. It consisted of nineteen stones, or words. They were: "But seek first the kingdom of God and his righteousness, and all these things will be added to you."

Now I owned two pieces of valuable jewelry. The necklace, truly, was more precious than, and preceded, the ring. But the necklace resembled the ring in that it pointed to the fact that I belonged to Someone – Someone Who loved me and had bought me with a very high price. As much as I could, I have shared that necklace. It clasped on easily and its weight was light. The strange part was that when I shared it, the strands of the necklace increased in beauty and added assurance to me.

43

Answered Prayer

Bless God in the great congregation, the LORD, O you who are of Israel's fountain!" There is Benjamin, the least of them, in the lead, the princes of Judah in their throng, the princes of Zebulun, the princes of Naphtali. Psalm 68:26-27

Benjamin, our fifth child, and born in 1978, was the only one of our children who came to see the light of day on a Sunday. The doctor had informed me, during a late term visit, that it would be a breech delivery. He also said that lying in a 'bum first' position during this last stretch of my pregnancy, the baby was not likely to change.

Tapping me on the stomach, the doctor smiled as he said: "It will, no doubt, be a difficult birth, Christine."

I was worried. I was so worried that my prayers became saturated with pleas.

"Please, Lord," I prayed on my knees in front of our bed, "if you help me to safely deliver this child, I will never ask you for anything else in my whole life."

Physically I was very uncomfortable. The baby lay straight across my belly. Feeling awkward and scared, I was happy my parents were due to visit a weekend close to my delivery date. The night before they came, I could not sleep. It was a Friday night and I left the confines of our warm bed to lumber around the living room. Nauseous and slightly unsteady, my stomach began to move convulsively and I lurched forward as the baby within me seemed in upheaval. The truth was that in those moments God turned Benjamin from the breech position he was in – turned him so that his little head, or big, if you will, locked down into the normal position in which he would be born.

The next day, a Saturday, much to the joy of the children, kind-hearted Opa and Oma Praamsma bought Kentucky Fried Chicken for supper. Labor began shortly after that meal as we were amiably conversing in the living room. I tried to catch Anco's eyes and signal that something was going on, but he fondly smiled back at me, thinking I was being romantic. I was not, and soon after my Dad and Mom had retired for the night, contractions slowed down. We reasoned that perhaps the Kentucky Fried Chicken had been the culprit and settled into bed, eventually falling asleep in the early morning hours. That sleep lasted until my water broke. When I nudged Anco and told him it was time to go to the hospital, he woke with such a start that he jumped out of bed, forgetting he was on the wall side. He banged his head so hard that he almost passed out and had to sit down for a moment before he could dress.

On the way to the hospital we stopped at the side of the road a few times, as we thought the baby might be born in the car. However, we did manage to reach the medical center before the birth. Our doctor, a man we knew because his children were in violin class with ours, was a short and rather docile man. (We later ascertained that he performed many abortions.) In any case, as I lay in the hospital bed, this doctor told me that the baby was ready to come out and that the only thing necessary for this to happen was for him to break the water. Now my water had broken at home. Suddenly enraged that this physician could not see that this had already occurred and what kind of doctor was he anyway, I sat up and yelled.

"Don't you touch me! Don't you touch me! Get away from me!"

Anco was alarmed and the obstetrician stepped backward, also alarmed. Anco came and stood right next to me.

"It's all right, sweetheart," he whispered, "The doctor can see the head coming and if he just breaks ...."

But that set me off again.

"My water already broke," I shouted at the top of my lungs, "and don't you let that man touch me."

"You probably had a double sac," he reasoned, "and really ...."

But I just kept on saying, "Anco, don't let that man touch me."

Eventually, worn out, I was done shouting, and lay down. The doctor did break the water, and Benjamin was born almost immediately. It was a Sunday morning.

There are apparently a range of hypothesized reasons for a double amniotic sac. One of these is that the pregnancy may have started as a multiple pregnancy, with one baby never developing to the fetal stage. Reabsorbed by the mother's body, this baby leaves behind an extra water sac.

Possibly our youngest was a twin. Perhaps, if this was so, this child has now met Anco, his earthly father.

44

Heartache

I am the LORD, and there is no other, besides Me there is no God; I equip you, though you do not know Me, that people may know, from the rising of the sun and from the west, that there is none besides Me; I am the LORD, and there is no other. I form light and create darkness; I make well-being and create calamity; I am the LORD, Who does all these things. Isaiah 45:5-7

Today I missed Anco so very much. The human being is meant to share – share not only meals and conversation, but also pain and sorrow. Oh, such sorrow I had today for someone much-loved who is cold and presently unwilling to extend love. Jeremiah's words in chapter 12:5-6 came to mind.

> If you have raced with men on foot, and they have wearied you, how will you compete with horses? And if in a safe land you are so trusting, what will you do in the thicket of the Jordan? For even your brothers and the house of your father, even they have dealt treacherously with you; they are in full cry after you; do not believe them, though they speak friendly words to you.

Oh, if only I could hide my face in Anco's jacket and sob. If only I could feel him patting my back and hugging me. But I know with a terrible certainty and emptiness in my heart that this will not be.

So I turn to the Bible and weep on it. I remember full well that Anco and I always prayed problems to the Lord –

whatever the problems would be – would pray them on our knees. Now I pray alone, but God will hear my single cry. I will pray according to His will and know that I will be comforted.

In Matthew 15 the woman with the demon-possessed daughter came to Jesus and begged Him to heal her child. The daughter, being demon-possessed, could not pray for herself. So her mother begged and pleaded with Jesus. "Heal my daughter! She is in such a state that she will not pray for healing for herself." The woman did not let up speaking for this child – she spoke for her child to the Lord. I know that speaking to God is a good thing. Did I myself not have a praying father and mother? Although parents can give neither children nor friends a new birth, they can pray for hard-heartedness to be softened, for stiff necks to bow and for enmity to turn to charity. Children of many prayers seldom perish. Even though Anco has gone ahead of me to heaven and even though I am alone for a while yet, I will persevere and not despair. The woman in the Bible professed she would be content with a few crumbs of mercy – and so will I.

Situations are never so useless that intercession for a loved one is of no avail. Satan would like despairing thoughts to rule; Satan would have melancholy grief strike me down.

What if I must pray for years? But Paul emboldened Christians to: "Pray without ceasing?" The woman in Matthew 15 prayed persistently and did not give up. And at the last she went home and found her daughter well.

My good friend Spurgeon advised: "Is there nothing to sing about today? Then borrow a song from tomorrow; sing of what is yet to be. Is this world dreary? Then think of the next." So I turn to the many friends who can comfort me between the pages of the Bible. I just have to keep turning the pages to find willing shoulders on which I may weep and smiling faces with whom I may rejoice.

45

False Teachers

But false prophets also arose among the people, just as there will be false teachers among you, who will secretly bring in destructive heresies, even denying the Master Who bought them, bringing upon themselves swift destruction. 2 Peter 2:1

Our children, all five of them, differed from one another. Where one was tenderhearted, another would be indifferent; where one was shy, the next one down might be confident; where one was fastidious another could be constantly untidy; where one was punctual, a sibling might very well be an eleventh-hour person. However, although their characteristics differed from one another, they all, like little teabags, were steeped in one infallible truth – that truth being the Bible. Anco and I endeavored to teach that Truth morning, noon and night. Through it we strove to hone virtues, excise vices and grow a vibrant love for their Lord and Savior.

In time our children went to school, even as Anco and I had gone to school. But we realized very soon that they, upon leaving the safe shelter of our home, were subject to the instructions and the philosophical systems of others. We tried very hard, therefore, to become acquainted with their teachers; tried to make sure that they had teachers who held to godly tenets.

Grade school was a Christian school. But the devil does not shun Christian schools. As a matter of fact, he has a predilection for them.

"Mom," one of my daughters informed me, leaning against the kitchen counter as she was eating her after-school snack, "our class is going to put on a Bible play and Mary gets to play the part of God. The teacher says that God can be a girl."

"What?" I said, not understanding properly, and sure I had not heard the information correctly.

"We're going to do a play," she repeated, "and Mary is going to play the part of God."

Anco suggested I phone the new part-time teacher. He was sure there had been a misunderstanding. The woman had, after all, been interviewed by the Education Committee. So phone her I did. However, as it turned out, perhaps because this new teacher had already taught at other Christian schools, no one had bothered to ask what the central beliefs which underpinned her faith were; everyone had taken for granted that she adhered to the precepts of the Scriptures.

"Hello."

The tone at the other end of the line was friendly.

"Hello, Mrs. Smith," I responded, slightly nervous, "my name is Christine Farenhorst and I think you are Emberlee's and Elineke's teacher. I'm their Mom."

"Oh."

The voice continued to be very friendly, adding, "Please call me Marj."

"All right, Marj," I went on, "please call me Christine."

So there we were, on a first name basis, and I was going to have to ask her some soul-searching questions.

"So what can I do for you?"

Her tone remained amiable and kind.

"Well, the girls told me that you were going to put on a play and I wanted to ask you about that."

"Yes, I am and I'm very excited about it. It'll be really good for the class and I hope to get everyone involved."

"It is good to get the kids involved," I proceeded hesitantly, "however, they told me that one of the parts in the play was ..." And I hesitated again, "was God."

"Yes, it is."

Marj was not one for avoiding issues, and I did appreciate her honesty. I cleared my throat.

"Do you not feel, Marj, that the holiness of God is a matter to be approached with great care and that playing-acting such a part would take away from that holiness."

"No, not at all," she responded, "As a matter of fact, it is good for a child to think more about God and to be able to play-act His character."

"As well," I continued, "there is the matter of gender. It seems to me ...."

She interrupted and laughed, "Oh, Christine, God could be a female, you know."

"The Bible teaches us differently, Marj," I answered, "and I'm afraid that I will have to broach this subject with the school board."

There was quiet at the other end of the telephone line. I was twisting the cord around my fingers.

"I suppose," she eventually said, "that you also believe that Jonah was swallowed by a whale and that Mary was a virgin? "

I swallowed. Where was all this coming from?

"I take it," I responded, "that you do not believe in the infallibility of the Bible."

"Oh, I believe the Bible teaches us many truths. But there are also things in it which we should read as an allegory, not as a literal truth."

"I see."

"Oh, Christine, let's be friends. I won't bother you about your literal beliefs and you should allow me the freedom to have my own thoughts."

"The trouble is, Marj," I slowly answered, "that your thoughts won't stop at your doorstep. They will enter my children's hearts and brains."

"Nonsense," she called out rather irritated, "I promise you that I will not impose my views on your children."

"You already have, Marj," I replied, "because they came home and told me about the play. They have already developed thoughts which you have planted in their minds."

The upshot of the matter was that Marj was not rehired. But this did not take place without disagreements within our church community and within the Christian school board. Many did not see the harm in Marj's point of view; many could not understand that she had both the paw of the lion and the paw of the bear and that her surname was Philistine. It was the beginning of many such battles fought on our doorstep; it was the beginning of years of unrest and disunity.

In the mid-1980s Howard Van Till's book *The Fourth Day* was published. It sought to reconcile Christianity with Darwinist science. Because Van Till was a teacher at Calvin College, the book received much publicity in the Christian Reformed Church. It was shocking for both Anco and myself to discover that most people in our church community had very little interest in defending biblical truth; and that the majority of fellow church members considered concerns regarding issues such as 'Women in Office', and 'homosexual relationships', as making mountains out of molehills. A liberalism which classified Christianity under the broad heading 'God is Love', had slipped into the pulpit.

My dear father, who died in 1984, had encouraged and schooled Anco during the years he attended McMaster, years in which he was inundated with evolutionary material in many science classes. As he pressed well-worn literature into our hands, literature written, for example, by Morris and Whitcomb, *(The Genesis Flood),* and Evan Shute, *(Flaws in the Theory of Evolution),* my father had prepared us for false teachers. Anco was convinced that the first few chapters of Genesis were pivotal in a sound faith life.

Although by nature both Anco and myself were peaceful persons, we believed that Luther's saying, "Peace if possible; truth at all costs," was required of us. And perhaps because he was a veterinarian, Anco also sided with Calvin who said: "A dog barks when his master is attacked. I would be a coward if I saw that God's truth is attacked and yet would remain silent."

By God's grace, our family was thrown into the cleansing cauldron of God's foundational doctrines known as the five

Solas: Sola Gratia – 'grace alone'; Sola Fide – 'faith alone'; Solus Christus – 'Christ alone'; Sola Scriptura – 'Scripture alone'; and Soli Deo Gloria – 'to the glory of God alone'.

46

Hearing and Speaking

My sheep hear My voice, and I know them, and they follow Me. John 10:27

God is a God Who listens, is slow to anger and abounding in steadfast love. Anco and I called Psalm 103 the Lord's Supper psalm because it was so often read during, or after, the Lord's Supper. Verse nine of this psalm says God will not always chide, nor will He keep His anger forever. This verse is a fundamental principle and a life-sustaining precept.

I have rarely met anyone who had the listening capability that Anco had. Often, during Bible study sessions or during conversations with our children, I marveled at the fact that he quietly sat back and simply listened – simply let people speak their mind. The words to which he listened could be slanderous, accusing, questioning, could go on ad infinitum, and even as I wound myself up considering all manner of reply, he would just seemingly relax and let people speak. Only when they were all done, totally exhausted by their spouting, would he respond in a calm and godly manner. It was a gift. I miss it and I hope that our children will strive to imitate it.

To be fair, this gift of listening grew on Anco – grew throughout the years – grew with increasing strong and steadfast faith – a gift of the Holy Spirit. It also grew by the example of godly fathers. Both Anco's father and my father had that same gift of listening. Anco learned from them as they exercised headship in their families, as they led in church fellowship and as they practiced the words they preached. But truly, Anco was first and foremost able to listen so well, because he himself listened to God's voice in the Bible.

There is a box with a stack of letters inside it on my night table next to the bed. They are filled with letters Anco wrote to me before we were married. He was not a letter-writing person and so I doubly appreciate these little epistles which he penned at least twice a week when I was not in the vicinity.

'My dearest Christine', or something akin to it, is written at the top of each letter. In the letter which I read today he was happy that we had been 'going steady' for six months and he expressed the sincere hope that we would be married for at least sixty-six years. Well, we didn't quite make that. But the wish was still heart-warming to read.

When Anco was still in high school and attending catechism, his pastor, Andy Kuyvenhoven, told him he should seriously consider the ministry. Anco did consider. It rather daunted him and in the end he opted for the task of caring for animals. And yet he never fully gave up thinking on the calling of pastor. As he aged, he grew more and more aware of the Great Commission. Studying the Bible diligently, he led many, many Bible studies. He rejoiced so in the message of salvation.

The saying that ministers should be 'called' is often highlighted. When we use this word we mean that candidates for the ministry should have a special desire to preach and shepherd, a desire placed there by the Lord. This is true. However, there are instances when the New Testament speaks of a calling for all of us. There are verses which do not refer to the filling of a pulpit each Sunday, but to the character of each Christian. Take Galatians 5:13 (NIV): "You, my brothers and sisters, were called to be free. But do not use your freedom to indulge the flesh; rather, serve one another humbly in love." Or, read I Peter 3:9 (NIV): "Do not repay evil with evil or insult with insult. On the contrary, repay evil with blessing, because to this you were called so that you may inherit a blessing."

We are, all of us, called to many things. Our behavior should always translate into godly demeanor, happy courtesy, meekness, and so on. We have all been called by God to follow His commands in a worthy manner, humility probably being the most important trait.

Anco was once asked by someone, someone who disliked him intensely, to come for a meeting in a Tim Horton's restaurant, so that she could speak with him. A very liberal woman, one who had wreaked havoc within the church community, she had also spread slander about him. He went and was reamed out in such a loud manner by this female, that people in surrounding booths turned their heads to look. It was embarrassing as well as demeaning. Anco listened quietly and let her go on and on. The woman ended the public diatribe by saying: "You are a narrow-minded bigot. It's like you're in a box and you don't allow anything else in that box." As she was sounding off this last statement, she drew the picture of a box on the booth table with her right index finger. Anco waited a moment to make sure she was done. Then he took his Bible and placed it in the box.

47

Treasure

For where your treasure is, there your heart will be also.
Matthew 6:21

All our children received music lessons. Making a joyful noise to the Lord was a daily business and we considered it a serious command. Strings and flute, we knew, were pleasing sounds to Him. Consequently, the boys had violin lessons, Emberlee and Elineke played the flute and Charity had a classical guitar. There were times when we literally shook our ceiling.

During the 1980s, Christopher's and Ben's violin teacher, Mrs. S, was phoned by a stranger to ask if she had any promising students. When the teacher asked why, the woman explained that she had a violin which she wanted to pass on to a child who thoroughly enjoyed playing and who exhibited talent. Mrs. S was kind enough to mention Christopher. That phone call resulted in a visit to our home one evening by a Hilda Rovikoff.

Hilda Rovikoff was in her seventies. When we opened the door after she knocked, we beheld a thin woman wearing a huge floppy hat. She also sported a baggy sweater over a black skirt and carried a very battered and worn violin case. It was the middle of winter and, therefore, when she took off her boots in the foyer, it amazed our whole family to see bare and gnarled feet emerge. Hilda kept her hat on as she casually padded into the living room and sat down on the couch.

"When I was a little girl," she told us, as our entire brood gathered around and listened wide-eyed and open-eared, "I was given this violin by someone with the stipulation that I give it to someone else when I was finished with it. My parents were not very well-to-do, so I was very grateful for the instrument. I've always played it with joy."

She then gave Christopher the violin case and asked him to open it, take out the violin and play for her. He looked at us questioningly, and we nodded. Opening up the dilapidated case, he carefully took out the violin. It was a beautiful instrument. A little nervous, he put it on his shoulder and began to play. Half-way through his piece, we could not help but notice that Hilda Rovikoff was crying. She was not just crying, she was sobbing. Christopher noticed it too, and missed a bar. We could see him thinking, "Am I playing this badly?" But he wasn't. And that's not why Hilda was crying. The woman was remembering. We could sense her reliving the moment decades and decades back when she had first received the violin; we could perceive that she was fully cognizant of that time in her life when the years were open and lay full of promise before her. Now she was an old woman, a widow with no children, and her time was almost done.

"When you are finished with the violin," she instructed Christopher after he had concluded his piece, "you must promise me that you will give it to someone else."

He promised and grinned. It was a wonderful violin with a rich mellow sound.

Hilda came back to visit us once again about six months later. This time she brought us a soup tureen and a silver butter dish.

"You are a large, happy family," she said, "and I'm sure you will eat from these things with love."

Then she asked Christopher to play for her once more and she cried again. We wrote to Hilda from time to time, but after a year or so, the letters came back with the word 'moved' stamped on it. We lost track – lost track until I read her obituary in the local newspaper.

I went to the funeral, piqued more by curiosity than by love. There were fifteen people, including myself, in the small funeral chapel. And most of these, I understood after talking to them, hadn't really known Hilda either. A woman who had lived across the hall from her delivered a small speech. Hilda had lived frugally, she told us, had donated (very nice) paintings to institutions and had gifted land to conservation authorities. Hilda, the acquaintance continued, never wanted to be praised for the gifts she rendered but waved aside all her generosity as a natural way of living that should be pursued by all people. Other neighbors – folk who had met her in passing – all liked her but no one knew whether or not she had been a Christian. The service was Anglican. Familiar liturgy was used: "Dust we are and to dust we will return," "The Lord is my Shepherd," and "For as in Adam all die, so in Christ shall all be made alive." Strangely enough, there was no singing. And then the casket was carried to the hearse.

I went home subdued. Spurgeon once said that every Christian is either a missionary or an imposter. Hilda had freely given away very precious things – things that meant the world to her. What was the most precious thing that Anco and I possessed? We spoke of it later and grew in knowledge – learning that having received freely, we should give freely.

PART IV:

CONTENTMENT IN GRIEF

48

Sleep

In peace I will lie down and sleep, for You alone, LORD, make me dwell in safety. Psalm 4:8 (NIV)

We were in the process of building a sunroom when Anco suffered his second stroke. Consequently, the house was in somewhat of a disrupted state at that time. It has since become more uncluttered and organized. I've been sleeping in our renovated bedroom for a week now. It's a cozy room. A bookcase stands on one side, the dresser next to it and the hope chest next to that. Anco made most of the things we used – our bed, our picture frames, the mug racks, the wall unit, stools, trays, and so on. I'm glad he did because all these items represent him, are part of him, and they surround me with his love.

Last Sunday in church a young man who attends our Bible study approached me and asked how I was doing.

"All right," I answered.

"Well, I know you've been having a rough go of it," he said, smiling at me, "and so I brought you a present."

He handed me a velvet bag and I fished out two beautiful wooden picture frames. One was made of blond wood and the other of oak. I loved both of them. They were well done and reminded me very much of Anco's beautiful, wood craftmanship. The frames also graciously exhibited the care of one Christian for another.

"You can only have one," he qualified and smiled.

So I chose the dark wood, the oak, and have put a picture into the frame of Anco and myself prior to our engagement. On that photograph, we appear very trusting and guileless.

The day before Anco's stroke there was a snow squall warning and our Bible study was canceled. In spite of the bad weather, that same young man came to our home. A conversation ensued around the kitchen table, a conversation about assurance of salvation. Anco, some five days prior to his death, was able to testify to the young fellow woodworker of his total trust in the Lord Jesus.

"I do not doubt," he attested, "but that I am saved. I feel it within every fiber of my being. God does not forsake the work of His hands."

Right now Anco is regarding me through that gifted, wooden picture frame. My dear husband, who at the time the picture was taken was less than twenty years old, looks innocent and young. And I, leaning against his shoulder on that picture, am presently very aware that both of us only endured because of the wooden frame of the Savior's cross – a frame which defined us.

49

All Creatures Great and Small

Not all flesh is the same: People have one kind of flesh, animals have another, birds another and fish another. 1 Corinthians 15:39 (NIV)

Psalm 50 tells us that every beast of the forest belongs to God and that He owns the cattle on a thousand hills. We are also informed in that same psalm that all the birds of the hills, and all that moves in the fields is valued by God.

Around 1980, we moved away from our little bungalow, moved half a kilometer down the road into a bigger house. Built for us by a friend, it was just a trifle closer to the clinic. Almost an acre big, we immediately began a garden and built a chicken coop. The building site was situated next to a Seventh Day Adventist church which was also in the process of being constructed. During our first month in the new house, we made a pact of sorts with the friendly sect next door. We promised that we would not mow the lawn during their Saturday church service, if they would promise not to run heavy machinery on the Lord's Day.

Anco and I have pretty well always kept animals in and around our home. This was perhaps a natural course of events because Anco was, after all, a veterinarian and he loved animals. Proverbs 12:10 tells us that a righteous man regards the life of his beast. Rabbits have hopped about in the backyard. Geese have pecked away at our vegetables and chickens have clucked in their coop. Java rice finches have sung to their heart's content in our living room in a beautifully crafted wooden cage and we have pictures of Dixie, one of our peacocks, sitting next to Spurgeon, our dog.

Visitors have not always appreciated the zoo-like quality of our living quarters. We owned one cat who had the strange but friendly habit of nuzzling ears. It was difficult, if not impossible, to break him of this habit. He used to sneak up some four or five feet behind people, take a flying leap and athletically land on someone's shoulder. A grey cat with a white streak running down his back, he was named Skunky.

One day Oma V called for tea. While she was sitting at the living room table, I was puttering around in the kitchen, arranging cookies on a plate and calling out if she wanted sugar and milk. Skunky was present on the floor behind her chair, meticulously washing himself. I carried a tray to the living room table and we had a cosy time of it, talking about the children, the weather and the church. The church topic was a bit touchy because Oma had not approved of our recent departure from the Christian Reformed Church. But she sipped her tea companionably and the conversation stayed affable. Suddenly Skunky decided the time had come for him to shoulder his responsibility as host. I didn't see him until he was in mid-air. Oma V had her teacup poised between the tablecloth and her mouth. The cup went flying. Red liquid shot up like a hot volcano. But it didn't shoot as high as Oma. I had no idea she had it in her.

"What's that?"

Her voice cracked as she yelped.

"Don't worry. It's just the cat," I soothed, also standing up.

Skunky immediately evacuated the scene of the crime. He didn't like noise. As I was reassuring Oma, offering more tea while I was mopping up the tablecloth, the ridiculousness of the situation came to me and tears of suppressed laughter jumped out of my eyes. I suddenly giggled and, having given way to my feelings, burst out into a great bellow of laughter. Fortunately, she laughed with me. Actually we both roared and I poured more tea.

About a week later, as all five of our children were gathered in a little group at the end of our driveway waiting for the school bus to pick them up, Skunky joined them. Tail up high, he crossed the road and seated himself across from them next to our mailbox. Watching everyone dolefully, he was cute but settled in a rather precarious spot. Cars passed frequently. Worried that he might cross the road while the bus was coming, Ben threw a stone towards him to make him run away. Not at all put out, Skunky turned playful. He swatted at the rock, bouncing it onto the road. Then he chased after it and an oncoming truck hit him before he knew what had happened. The bus arrived at this precise point from the opposite direction, and all five children boarded. The bus left, exposing the little lifeless body of Skunky as it lay by the mailbox. The whole scene had played out in less than half a minute. Horrified I had watched from the living room window. My next action was to race to the phone to call Anco. By the time he answered, I was fairly incoherent. Finally able to decipher that none of his children had been killed, he was not particularly upset by the passing of our little feline. But he did come home to scoop up Skunky, bury him in the back field and give me a hug and a kiss.

Isaiah 11 was one of our favorite passages. It gives the promise of the restoration of all people, it speaks of the Christ coming from the stump of Jesse, it foretells a future in which evil will be abolished and only peace will be present.

> The wolf shall dwell with the lamb, and the leopard shall lie down with the young goat, and the calf and the lion and the fattened calf together; and a little child shall lead them. The cow and the bear shall graze; their young shall lie down together; and the lion shall eat straw like the ox. The nursing child shall play over the hole of the cobra, and the weaned child shall put his hand on the adder's den. They shall not hurt or destroy in all my holy mountain; for the earth shall be full of the knowledge of the LORD as the waters cover the sea. (vs. 6-9)

I find increasing joy in the fact that, away from this present, ever-escalating violent society, where not only kittens are hit by oncoming trucks, but children are hit by lying woke culture and indecent moral codes, Anco is now personally privy to the reality of this passage and surely rejoicing in the arms of his Father, the everlasting Prince of Peace.

50

Running Towards Joy

You make known to me the path of life; in Your presence there is fullness of joy; at Your right hand are pleasures forevermore. Psalm 16:11

Anco and I loved old paintings, especially the Old Masters. We spent hours in the Rijksmuseum in Amsterdam when we visited Holland in the 1990s, enjoying Vermeer, Rembrandt, Jan Steen, and others. We also visited Belgium and toured churches to admire Peter Paul Rubens' masterpieces. At home, Anco enjoyed crafting picture frames into which we hung some of these paintings, albeit only copies.

There is a painting by the prolific Swiss artist, Eugéne Burnand, (1850-1921), in which he depicts the disciples Peter and John running at breakneck speed towards the open grave. Peter, the impetuous one, has his hair flying behind his head, so eager is he to reach the tomb. The Gospel of John tells us, however, that John, full of faith, outran Peter.

It is possible to place yourself into Burnand's biblical painting, as indeed, you can place yourself into many depictions of Bible truths. For example, we can, and maybe should, see ourselves in 'The Fall of Man', as we contemplate a painting on that subject by Peter Brueghel; as well, we can conceivably shudder upon seeing the horrendously high waves detailed in various interpretations of the worldwide flood; we also might take our place alongside Abraham as he trudges up to Mount Moriah when we study Caraveggio's 'The Sacrifice of Isaac'; and when we see illustrations of Elijah lying under the broom tree, we might perchance see a mirror image of ourselves when we are tired and when we are afraid that dangers might to overcome us.

When I view Burnand's painting of the disciples, or when I read John's account of this marathon, I realize that I myself am also running towards the open tomb of the Lord – running as if my life depended on it. Because it does. I can actually run to the Bloomingdale Mennonite Cemetery, where Anco is buried, from my house. It is not difficult to physically do so. The two men running in the picture in Bernand's painting are running on the first day of the week – on a Sunday – a day in which we ought to run to church.

The Apostles' Creed, a creed which summarizes the Gospel, confesses:

> I believe in God the Father, Almighty, Maker of heaven and earth.
> And Jesus Christ, His only begotten Son, our Lord, Who was conceived by the Holy Spirit, born of the virgin Mary;
> Suffered under Pontius Pilate; was crucified, dead, and was buried; He descended to hell;
> The third day He rose again from the dead;
> He ascended to heaven, and is seated at the right hand of God the Father almighty.
> From thence He shall come to judge the living and the dead.
> I believe in the Holy Spirit,
> I believe a holy catholic church, the communion of saints,
> The forgiveness of sins,
> The resurrection of the body,
> And the life everlasting. Amen.

The third and fourth articles of this Creed prod me to run with Peter and John. Suffered under Pontius Pilate; was crucified, dead, and was buried; He descended to hell; The third day He rose again from the dead; Jesus died for my sins, was buried and rose again. He is the firstfruits of many – the firstfruits of my father, of my mother, of my dear husband, Anco, and of all those who come running in faith to the empty tomb.

There have always been people who ran in faith towards the empty tomb. Sabina Wurmbrand, (1913-2000), related stories in her book *The Pastor's Wife*, of many such runners. One of these runners is a young girl, a girl who shared a prison cell with Sabina Wurmbrand in Communist Romania. This girl, the daughter of an important Communist official, had become a Christian and was, consequently, imprisoned for her faith. Often imprisoned people in these cells were shot by a firing brigade with very little warning, if any, that they were about to die. The young girl was notified one evening that she would be shot at midnight. She partook of her last meal, which consisted of watery oatmeal, calmly. "Soon," she told the other prisoners in her cell, "my body will return to dust. Perhaps grass will grow out of it. But there is much more to death than the decay of my body. It is my soul which will directly go to God's Kingdom."

When the girl was taken by the guards at midnight, she began reciting the Apostles' Creed. Her voice echoed and re-echoed through the stone-walled corridors as she walked by the cells. And every sentence, every article, took on poignant meaning for those she passed. Every word was wrung from a suffering, but also a rejoicing, heart. The girl knew that she was dying for the one true God, and that she was running towards an open tomb. She was aware that she was sharing in Jesus' suffering and that she would also share in His glory.

I can feel the wind in my hair as I run. It feels so good and in the distance I can see the rock rolled away from the entrance to the tomb. The days melt away under the pounding of my feet. Oh, death, where is your sting? Oh, grave, where is your victory?

51

The Raccoon

The fear of you and the dread of you shall be upon every beast of the earth and upon every bird of the heavens, upon everything that creeps on the ground and all the fish of the sea. Into your hand they are delivered. Genesis 9:2

Although we always, throughout our many years of living in the country, have had various domestic pets both for enjoyment as well as for food purposes, there was one animal which plagued us. This animal was the raccoon. Cute, with a mask-like countenance, it bit, and loved to kill, our chickens.

Anco and I contemplated the phrase in Genesis 9:2, and came across an explanation of it by a John Gill, (1697-1771), Baptist pastor of the Metropolitan Tabernacle in London. He wrote:

> This is a renewal, at least in part, of the grant of dominion to Adam over all the creatures; these obeyed him cheerfully, and from love. But sinning, Adam in a good measure lost his power over them. They rebelled against him. But now, though the charter of power over them is renewed, they do not serve man freely, but are in dread of him, and flee from him. Some are more easily brought into subjection to him, and even the fiercest and wildest of them may be tamed by him; and this power over them was the more easily retrieved in all probability by Noah and his sons, from the inhabitation of the creatures with them for so long a time in the ark. (John Gill's Exposition of the Old Testament)

For a while we thought of taping John Gill's explanation to the chicken coop fence, but then remembered that raccoons do not read. We raised chickens, mostly egg-layers and, at times, meat birds as well. Raccoons are not vegetarians and seemed to have a special affinity for our chickens. Presuming our coop to be a drive-through, fast-food facility, they have, time and again, eaten and run.

Coming home from church one evening, Anco, dressed in his Sunday clothes, was so incensed by a raccoon lurking about the coop that he chased the animal up a tree situated right next to the pen. The raccoon, being the better climber, made it to the top of the tree in record time, still clutching a chicken. The chicken cackled loudly and insistently and then suddenly stopped. It was a sturdy tree and Anco made it to the second limb quite easily. But it was a dark night and when he looked up through the leafy branches above him, although he heard the thieving mammal hissing and grunting, he could not see it. So standing up on the second limb, he began to shake the tree as hard as he could. Anger can create a power surge and the tree shook like an aspen in a violent storm. Nothing happened initially, and stopping to better assess the situation, Anco peered up again only to receive a bleeding and dead fowl smack in the face and chest.

A trap was set out faithfully each night. We tempted the raccoon with corn, carrots and baked goods for a long time to no avail. Sooner or later, we thought, the animal will succumb to the temptations in the cage and be caught.

A few days later, again arriving home on a pitch-dark night from a meeting and checking the coop, Anco ascertained that the raccoon had, at long last, been caught in the cage. Lifting it up, he submerged the trap into a large drum of water. Then he came in, recounted his victory with a smile, before crawling into bed next to me. He slept soundly. In the morning, he retrieved the cage, fully expecting to find a drowned coon. He was unpleasantly surprised, however, to discover that he had drowned one of our own chickens.

It was that same summer, again on an evening, that Anco and I heard a noise on the back porch.

"The coon is in the compost pail," Anco said in a low tone, getting up from his chair, "and I'm going to get him this time."

Now we had in our possession an Australian club said to be used by aborigines when hunting. This instrument was hastily appropriated from the hall closet by Anco. I was then instructed by him to station myself by the back door.

"Turn on the outside light and open the door at the same time," he whispered.

Our compost pail was situated on our deck right around the corner of the back door.

"Ready?" my husband mouthed, as he crouched down next to me, club in his right hand.

Opening the rear entrance quickly, I switched on the porch light and Anco promptly moved onto the deck. The next moment the lid of the compost pail clattered onto the ground with small thuds. Then Anco reappeared inside, clutching the club. He had a strange look on his face.

"It's a ...," he said, and then, interrupting himself, spoke rather sharply, "Shut the door! Shut the door!"

I complied and the back entry banged shut.

"The lid was half-off," Anco disclosed, "and as I bent down, ready to hit the raccoon, I suddenly realized I was looking straight into the face of a skunk."

We regarded each other for a moment before the absurdity of the whole situation hit us. Indeed, we began to laugh so hard that hilarity vibrated off the kitchen walls. Then, recollecting ourselves, we both ran for the open windows, closing every single one of them. It didn't much help. We still had to sleep in the basement that night.

I don't remember if we ever caught that particular raccoon. The beasts over which man was given dominion, include the raccoon. But in the post-sin world, this will be a continual struggle until the end of time.

52

Letters

Are we beginning to commend ourselves again? Or do we need, as some do, letters of recommendation to you, or from you? You yourselves are our letter of recommendation, written on our hearts, to be known and read by all. And you show that you are a letter from Christ delivered by us, written not with ink but with the Spirit of the living God, not on tablets of stone but on tablets of human hearts. 2 Corinthians 3:1-3

I was reading some old letters tonight – letters Anco wrote to me the first year we went out together. I don't read one of these letters every night but save them for a time that is special. These old letters, ones from years ago, are heartening, supportive and they evoke all sorts of memories.

The summer of 1966, the time that some of these letters were written, I was working in Toronto. My sister Johanna had given birth to a second baby and I was a full-time nanny for her as she worked. Anco often came over for weekends. In between, we sent lots of letters to one another – three or four a week – and I was devastated when the mailman did not stop by with an envelope in his pouch for me.

What if he could write me a letter now? Wouldn't that be something? Imagine getting a letter from heaven in the mailbox at the end of the driveway! I would be overjoyed with just one letter a month now, or one a year, or just one letter. In my heart I often write messages to Anco, telling him about minor matters, including problems that crop up. I do so miss having his down-to-earth evaluation of petty arguments, his reassuring voice telling me that minor matters which so easily snowball into boulders, are 'nonsense'.

About two thousand years have passed since Moses and Elijah spoke with Jesus on the Mount of Transfiguration. They were dressed in recognizable bodies and came to speak with Jesus. These men were letters of encouragement to Him. John, Peter and James saw and heard Jesus speak with these Old Testament figures and, as a result, they were motivated in faith as well. The encouragement given to Jesus by Moses and Elijah is so very necessary for me also, for He was about to be crucified for my salvation.

In actuality there is no need for any visual letter from Anco. The memory of the grace and faith in his life is a letter written, not with ink, but with the Spirit of the living God.

I would like to tell Anco that we have seven great grandchildren. I would like to ask him if he remembers the cradle he made for our firstborn. And I would like to reminisce about all our five treasures who slept in that cradle. And I hear him whisper, "They were never ours to keep, Christine. We were simply allowed to water them a bit as they grew."

A small anecdote related by William Barclay speaks of growth. In this anecdote the story of a church in London is recounted. The time it takes place is during the Second World War.

Prior to a Thanksgiving service, the members of the congregation had placed harvest gifts in front of the sanctuary, including a sheaf of corn. The Thanksgiving service, however, was never celebrated because the Saturday evening before that service, there was an air raid and the church was hit. The place of worship was totally demolished and lay in sorry ruins. Nevertheless, that following spring, on the bomb site where the church had stood, shoots of green appeared in the broken cement. Notwithstanding the bombing, and in spite of the sinful intent of the devil, those shoots flourished and the following months saw corn stalks grow. They were tall stalks and towered over the rubble.

I would venture to say that there are many letters of recommendation written all around us, if only we would open our eyes to read them.

53

Dinner Conversations

On this mountain the LORD of hosts will make for all peoples a feast of rich food, a feast of well-aged wine, of rich food full of marrow, of aged wine well refined. And He will swallow up on this mountain the covering that is cast over all peoples, the veil that is spread over all nations. He will swallow up death forever; and the Lord GOD will wipe away tears from all faces, and the reproach of His people He will take away from all the earth, for the LORD has spoken. It will be said on that day, "Behold, this is our God; we have waited for Him, that He might save us. This is the LORD; we have waited for him; let us be glad and rejoice in His salvation." Isaiah 25:6- 9

Gerry was a friend whom we often had over for dinner. To the best of our knowledge, he was not a believer. Anco had met Gerry at a local chess tournament. Sensing the man was lonely, in a moment of compassion he had invited him over for dinner. In the months and years that followed, Gerry became a frequent guest. A university graduate who had once been a high school teacher, he was neither well-to-do nor accustomed to bathing regularly. When we came to know him, the wiry, little man was the rather musty owner of an antique shop and an enthusiast of old books and stamps. Living from hand to mouth, Gerry had only a small circle of acquaintances and could be considered somewhat of a hermit.

Each time we had Gerry over for dinner, he would habitually say, "The only thing wrong with you folks is that you are Christians." And then he would smile, as if to apologize for the comment. When Anco opened in prayer before meals, the antiquarian often made a lot of noise by opening the medicine bottles stowed away in his pockets. These contained heart pills, lactose-intolerance pills and pills for his Crohn's disease. When the 'Amen' was pronounced the pills lay next to his plate and his fork was ready in his hand to begin eating. There was no doubt that Gerry loved dining with us and that he especially delighted in dessert time.

After we ate, it was our custom to read a portion of Scripture. Anco and I always read a passage together, taking turns to read two verses each. Gerry never made any protest. He leaned back in his chair, folded his arms across his chest, and conveyed the impression that he was listening. But after the reading, he inevitably uttered some remark, always pronouncing a verdict about how ridiculous it was to believe in a God Who created the world simply by the word of His mouth; and strangely, no matter what we read, he would be moved to throw in a sarcastic comment on the parting of the Red Sea.

"The Bible was not the first book written, you know," he would say, and grin at the same time, "Moses was only copying some of the stories from ancient people who lived before him. And actually, the Israelites did not cross the Red Sea, but the Reed Sea. It was dry already. It's all myth and legend. You people are not in the real world. You're not aware of what science has discovered."

It did not matter to Gerry what we said in response to his sentiments or analyses. He would always succumb to the human notion that it was impossible to believe in a God Who could speak and create; in a God Who was so mighty and vast that it overpowered all thought; in a God Who was totally in control of all things.

"Have you never heard of Darwin?" he would interject from time to time, waving his hand across his plate as he spoke.

We loved Gerry, and Anco especially, prayed for him continually.

Gerry did attend Sunday school as a child. He told us this a number of times. But he was convinced that Bible stories did not have to be believed literally. The nub of faith, to him, was that there was a God somewhere, that loving one's neighbor was good, and that you did your best.

"I'm not an atheist," Gerry told us several times, "I'm an agnostic. There might be a God. I'm not opposed to the thought. And if there is, He will know I've done my best."

"There is no such animal, Gerry, as an agnostic," Anco would reply with a laugh, "There is no fence-sitting. Either you believe, or you don't."

Gerry, who plied me with antiquarian things and fusty-smelling books from his antique shop when he came over, was always welcomed by us. We loved him. And, with our dinner conversations ringing in his ears, he died in a hospital bed, of heart problems.

Anco and I heard an anecdote once of a young woman who was diagnosed with a terminal illness. She phoned her pastor and wanted to meet with him to discuss certain aspects of her funeral service – songs that were to be sung and Scriptures that were to be read. He came to her home and spoke with her about these last wishes. As he was getting ready to leave, she mentioned to him one final aspect of the service – she wished to be buried with a fork in her right hand. Puzzled, the pastor asked her why she wanted this. She explained:

"When I attended social dinners during my life, after the dishes of the main course were being cleared away from the table, someone would usually say, 'Keep your fork'. It was my favorite part of the dinner, because I knew that something better was coming, something like chocolate cake, or deep-dish apple pie. Something wonderful!! So, I just want people to see me lying in my casket with a fork in my hand and I want them to wonder, 'What's with the fork?' Then I want you, my pastor, to tell them this story: that the best is yet to come!"

54

In The Ark

Where can I go from Your Spirit? Where can I flee from Your presence? If I go up to the heavens, You are there; if I make my bed in the depths, You are there. If I rise on the wings of the dawn, if I settle on the far side of the sea, even there Your hand will guide me, Your right hand will hold me fast. If I say, "Surely the darkness will hide me and the light become night around me," even the darkness will not be dark to You; the night will shine like the day, for darkness is as light to You. For You created my inmost being; You knit me together in my mother's womb. I praise You because I am fearfully and wonderfully made; Your works are wonderful, I know that full well. Psalm 139:7-14 (NIV)

I hear snow/rain/sleet particles hit the window next to my bed. Anco and I would often pretend on those occasions when we heard the sound of rain on the window, that we were in the ark. We would incontrovertibly know that although all outside was chaos, storms could not touch us. It was a comforting thought and I would grinningly call him Noah and he would respond by calling me Mrs. Noah.

Now I hear the precipitation, but there is no one with me to share these reassuring ideas. But the truth is, of course, that I am safe in the ark. That is a sure thing.

When I was a little girl, my mother taught me how to knit. She had patience and I produced row upon row of straight and purl, straight and purl creations. My light brown teddy bear was beautifully and warmly dressed. That is what I proudly thought as I held up what I imagined were fine aprons, skirts and hats. I fancied myself a small, female Michaelangela in progress. Often I did not notice the stitches I had dropped in my hurry to produce a garment, nor did I think it important to dwell on possible future holes in my bear's toggery. My mother, however, always unraveled. She pulled out row upon row of the straight and purl I had sweated over and she unfailingly instructed me to redo them.

Would that there was such an easy solution to problems! Would that we could simply unravel circumstances. Live backwards, as it were, and fix the gaping holes time produced. But the rows upon rows of sorrowful events that line the months and years of the past cannot, generally speaking, be undone. Often there are the Chaldeans, the Sabeans, the dead sheep, the lost fortunes, the broken health issues, the derision of others, and the graves. These are all holes in the past, gaping pits with wide open mouths. They cannot be undone.

There are past creations without holes also. I guess they can be called 'blessed memories'. I can run my hand over the crocheted bedspread covering of our bed. My hand can caress row upon row of colored lines upon which I worked years ago as I sat in the living room or in the study with Anco nearby. Perhaps this row was crocheted, I think, when Anco played a game of chess with a friend; perhaps this row was produced just before he turned away from his desk, smiled, and said: "Sweetheart, let's play a game of boggle;" perhaps this piece of wool heard him sigh as he bent over troublesome consistory notes; and, perhaps in this row, he caught my eye, winked at me and came over to give me a kiss.

Either way, the truth is that we can't go back in time. Neither can we stop time. When we peer over our shoulders, there will always be times of mourning next to times of dancing; when we remember the past, we unfailingly see times of war neighboring times of peace. But when we remember these times from the perspective of the ark, there is a closing of holes and a refuge from storm and chaos.

I was knit together in my mother's womb. The Master Craftsman Who spoke the world and everything in it into being, fashioned me and never dropped a stitch. Though I may be pursued by men, though my flesh may seem to shrivel, He does not have to redo my frame. For from before the foundation of the world, He planned my form. I need fear neither gaping hole nor coffin pit. For my Maker is my husband and I am convinced that after my skin has been destroyed, I will see God in my flesh. How my heart yearns within me!!

55

You Became Mine

When I passed by you again and saw you, behold, you were at the age for love, and I spread the corner of My garment over you and covered your nakedness; I made My vow to you and entered into a covenant with you, declares the Lord GOD, and you became Mine. Ezekiel 16:8

To be married in the Lord is surely a blessing. God blessed Anco and me richly in that He gave us almost fifty-three years of marriage. Added to that, he blessed us with five children and twenty-nine grandchildren – all of them, as much as can be discerned with the human eye, within His covenant. He is a faithful God, a gracious God and we praised His most holy and wonderful name for these gifts.

We met, Anco and I, through the providence of God, in 1963. I had just moved back to Ontario with my father and mother after living in Grand Rapids, Michigan for a year. It was the eighth time I had changed schools, and I was an awkward, unhappy and shy grade ten student all of fifteen years old.

We first saw one another, Anco and I, in a math home room at Hamilton District Christian High School. I remember thinking that the dark-haired boy was nice and that 'Anco' was a rather unusual name. Gradually acclimatizing to the Canadian high school system into which I had been thrown half-way through grade ten, I managed to pass, (with my Dad coaching me in Latin at home). In grade eleven, Anco began to exhibit some active interest in me by giving me candies as we knelt down in the school hall taking books out of our lockers. Slightly sweaty, these candies had phrases printed on them – phrases such as "I love you" and "I give you my heart." But these phrases were in Dutch and I rather doubt that Anco knew the exact meaning of them. His Mom put them in his lunch and he passed them on to me. I also remember being in awe of Anco's prowess in football, physics, chemistry, and math. As a matter of fact, he was one of the smartest boys I had ever known. He was also handsome and always smiled at me when he walked past, and, at the grade eleven year-end class party, tried very hard to sit next to me.

We began to date the first week of grade twelve, just prior to my seventeenth birthday. My parents thought I was much too young to date and, looking back, I do see we were virtual babies in the 'love' department. But one thing stands out in my mind regarding our relationship – that is that from the beginning of our friendship we were able to pray together. Our hands entwined and our hearts bowed down, we brought our concerns and thanks to God. Four and a half years later, we married.

It still floors me again and again to think of how marvelously good God has been towards us. It would be untrue to say that Anco and I never had arguments, problems, worries or sorrows. We had more than our share of them and they ranged from trivial to signficant. Such things as smelly feet in bed, car troubles, financial hardships, cancer and the death of our beloved parents, were just a few of the matters with which we grappled.

As early as the seventies, the decade into which our five children were born, a pot of troublesome concoctions was set to boil and then simmer on the back-burner of the Christian Reformed Church's synodical ovens. These concoctions included matters of Genesis interpretation and the ordination of women to office. In the very early nineties, another condiment was added to the already extremely unpleasant broth stewing within the denomination – that of loose methods of the interpretation of certain texts in Scripture, including those regarding homosexual behavior. The upshot of the resulting spiritual food was: "Did God really say?" It left us sick at heart.

Strangely enough, although the Word of God was watered down in many pulpits, this visible bruising of the church became a blessing to our family. It was as if Joseph said to us: "Others mean this for evil, but God means this for your good, to bring about that many people should be kept alive .... So do not fear: I will provide for you and your little ones." And God did provide for us. The slippery slope exhibited within the church proved to be the tilt that caused our family to climb up and study God's Word in such a way as we never would have done had there been no issues. Consequently, our children were taught male headship by both Scripture and by Anco's example; they were grounded in the fact that God hates all sexual sin; and they were spoon-fed on the historicity and infallibility of the Bible.

God did, indeed, enter into a covenant relationship with our family.

56

Upheld

Thus says the LORD: "Let not the wise man boast in his wisdom, let not the mighty man boast in his might, let not the rich man boast in his riches, but let him who boasts boast in this, that he understands and knows Me, that I am the LORD who practices steadfast love, justice, and righteousness in the earth. For in these things I delight, declares the LORD." Jeremiah 9:23-24

I was reading Matthew 17 today – mulling over the fact that after the Transfiguration, Jesus came down from the mountain and that the crowd was overwhelmed with wonder when they saw Him. Never before had I pondered or thought deeply about that particular phrase "overwhelmed with wonder when they saw Jesus." Perhaps His face was still shining; perhaps His countenance was full of compassion and love.

These people at the foot of the mountain, including the nine disciples, were obviously helpless when left on their own. Their problem was the child, the boy afflicted with convulsions, the one they could not heal.

I think I sometimes suffer spiritual convulsions. And these convulsions throw me to the ground in weakness. They make me question whether things will ever be the same again. I foam at the mouth and thrash about, not knowing what I am thinking or doing. All this while Jesus is on the Mount of Transfiguration. During this time, people hover about me. They marvel at the seeming hopelessness and sadness of my situation. They doubt my sanity. But then, when they are ready to pronounce me dead, Jesus comes down from the mountain. I do not even see Him, cannot even approach Him of my own volition, cannot even reach out to Him. No!! It is He Who sees me; it is He Who takes me by the hand; and it is He Who lifts me up. Much to the wonderment of the others, I live. I stand because Jesus has taken me by the hand. I am alive because He has made me so.

Even so in my sorrow, as I flounder about on the ground, even as I forget to look up, my Lord, the One Who intercedes for me, takes me by the hand each day.

Every part of each day I need to remember that in my own flesh I can do nothing; that without Jesus, I will be a failure. But with Him holding my hand, I can stand. Every one of my actions, if I rely on Him, is not a lonely endeavor. His hand will always lift me up, for He exercises steadfast love, justice, kindness and mercy towards His children and I am His child at the foot of the Mount of Transfiguration.

57

Some of the Peoples

After this I looked, and behold, a great multitude that no one could number, from every nation, from all tribes and peoples and languages, standing before the throne and before the Lamb, clothed in white robes, with palm branches in their hands, and crying out with a loud voice, "Salvation belongs to our God Who sits on the throne, and to the Lamb! And all the angels were standing around the throne and around the elders and the four living creatures, and they fell on their faces before the throne and worshiped God saying, "Amen! Blessing and glory and wisdom and thanksgiving and honor and power and might be to our God forever and ever! Amen." Revelation 7:9-12

A number of years ago, Anco and I had the privilege of visiting Colorado, a US state encompassing most of the Southern Rocky Mountains. Its diverse geography ranges from alpine plains and deserts to canyons, sandstone and rock formation, rivers and lakes. It's the only state that lies above 1000 meters elevation. Our specific destination was Colorado Springs where our daughter, Emberlee, and her family were living for a few months.

Colorado Springs stands at 6,035 feet above sea level which is probably why we felt keen pressure in our heads, a feeling much like a severe headache. We were told that the cure consisted in drinking lots of water. So armed with water bottles, we ventured out on day trips and encountered some wondrous miracles of God's creation in this area surrounded by desert and mountains.

Unquestionably, one of the most memorable trips we took was one on Phantom Canyon Road, a road which follows the path of an old railroad. This road, built more than a hundred years ago, connected the Colorado gold mining towns of Cripple Creek and Viktor to the outside world. The rutty, gravel route increases in elevation from 5,500 to 9,500 feet, and its extreme narrowness and ess curves stopped my heart several times. The scenery was breathtaking, but the road itself was very rough with no place on the single lane for another vehicle to pass. This continually caused Anco and me to wonder what would happen if we were to meet one along a sheer cliff edge. Prayer consequently arose simultaneously with gasps of incredulity at the spectacular views. Along the way, two tunnels cut through vast mountains, amazing rock formations lined the road, while below, (always below), chasms stretched. It was not a path for the faint of heart. A natural habitat for mountain lion, black bear and bobcat, of whom we only saw pawprints, the drive filled us with awe and respect for our Creator. Everywhere there were signs of the upheaval of the Great Flood that His hand had caused, while at the same time we sensed His hand upholding a diverse and grand creation.

During the days that followed, Anco and I also visited the Cheyenne Zoo, the Will Rogers Shrine, hiked in several state parks and strolled through the Colorado Fine Arts Center. Strangely enough, or perhaps not so strange, was the fact that all these things were not the most memorable events of our trip.

An old, eighty-something female volunteer at an information center in Manitou Springs, a small tourist town abutting Colorado Springs, was sweeping the parking lot when we drove in one day.

"Welcome! Welcome!" she cried out, "How are you folks doing?"

When she found out that we were from Canada, she waved us inside the building, all the while smiling and telling us how pleased she was to see us. Later, as we returned, laden with brochures, she told us that she was a Christian and that Christ was her Savior.

While driving towards the small town of Calhan after visiting a wildlife center, we encountered a stranded pick-up truck by the side of the road. A kilometer further, a burly looking man, flanked by a boy, strode along purposefully, toting an orange gerry can. We stopped and offered them a ride to the nearest gas station. They were extremely grateful. As we drove them back to their car with a full gas can, the father, a septic tank cleaner, told us that he loved to go to church and hear the Word preached.

The proprietress of a Subway franchise was rather reticent as she prepared a salad. But she wore a necklace on which hung both a shark and a cross. When questioned, she told us that her mother had given it to her.

"Someone came in here the other day," she informed us, as she scooped up the salad ingredients, "and was upset with me for wearing this necklace. 'How can you wear a shark and a cross at the same time?' was what the person said. But I told her that sharks are great animals who clean up the ocean and that God made the shark, and that's that!"

And she handed us our salad.

The owner of a tourist shop was playing godly music. When we asked if he was a Christian, he smiled.

"Yes, I am," he answered, "and this is what the wife and I do to pass on God's message."

On our way home, a black lady vendor at the Denver airport sold me a banana. It was very early in the morning and I asked her at what time she'd had to crawl out of her warm bed that morning. She replied that 3:00 a.m. was her usual time.

"I don't mind," she shrugged, "because this is when I have my prayer – my devotion time. And even when I don't have to get up early for work, I'm so used to it that I do it anyway."

She had a friendly grin and went on to tell us that she relied on God for everything and that she couldn't make it through a single day without Him.

Although the physical beauties of Colorado Springs and the surrounding area were amazing – including the colony of prairie dogs we watched, the black-billed magpies who were everywhere, the mule-deer with their white tails, the gigantic cottonwoods, the geese with their goslings, the herons, and so on – these were not the ultimate attractions of our visit. The truly most amazing and most memorable event of this trip was the light we saw shining in the hearts of other pilgrims – the light of the knowledge of the glory of God in the face of Jesus Christ.

Anco is now a very real part of that great multitude of pilgrims which no man can number. He is standing before God's throne and before the Lamb, clothed in a white robe. And he is singing to his Creator God and the words of his mouth are pure, clear and forceful and they echo throughout heaven: "Salvation belongs to our God who sits upon the throne, and to the Lamb!"

It used to be that, as a child, I would stand on my head the night before we went on holidays. I would be so excited that I could not sleep and out of sheer delight with the prospect of going away with my father and mother, I would kick off the covers on my bed and stand on my head at the foot of the bed. It is something I physically do not attempt any longer, but the excitement and anticipation of a holy time still churns my stomach. Oh, how I long to stand before that throne myself and sing along.

58

Cast Down

Why are you cast down, O my soul, and why are you in turmoil within me? Hope in God; for I shall again praise Him, my salvation and my God. Psalm 42:11

Today I was sure that something I had prayed for earnestly had come to pass. I cried in thankfulness. But then, as it turned out, my request did not come to pass.

Hebrews 11 is a wonderful and encouraging chapter in the Bible. "By faith .... by faith .... by faith" .... The words are hammered into us again and again, as if we are nails that will not enter wood.

The apple of God's eye, the Israelites, fled through the Red Sea and arrived safely on the other side. The Egyptians, whose hearts were hardened, raced through the same sea, but they were drowned. The Israelites marched around Jericho and it fell. The people in Jericho prayed to idols and were destroyed.

Was my feeble prayer a distrustful fleeing through the Red Sea? Were my hoarse cries a doubt-filled marching around Jericho? Should I stop praying? Spurgeon once said: "Anything is a blessing which makes us pray," and I know that Jesus sometimes lets us wait for that which we pray in His name, but He will never disappoint us or be untrue to His own words. I have the example of my father, who was always found on his knees in front of his bed the first thing every morning. I have the example of my husband who consistently brought his needs to God.

The only thing I have to do when troubled, lonely or disillusioned, even by those closest to me, is simply take God's hand and believe that the waves and breakers that sweep over me will be directed away. I only have to take God's hand and take faltering baby steps through the Red Seas and around the Jerichos that stand between myself and Canaan. "Out of my distress I called on the LORD; the LORD answered me and set me free. The LORD is on my side; I will not fear. What can man do to me?" Through the Holy Spirit, Psalm 118:5-6 reaffirms what I know deeply within myself.

Anco and I knew a beekeeper who lived not too far away from us when we still resided in Owen Sound. He was a burly fellow, a Netherlander, who had a heart full of kindness and who loved singing. The man had lost a teenage son due to a car accident and would weep when speaking of this child. He suffered from a bad hip and painfully hobbled about on a pair of crutches. As he grew older, he began exhibiting signs of dementia. We visited him from time to time, sat with him by the kitchen table, drank tea and chatted. We spoke of Jesus, of God's great love and of the blessings He showered on us. John, for that was his name, was skeptical but also frantic in his search for peace.

"He does not hear me," he cried out, banging his fist on the table, "and I am alone. My wife does not love me and she will, sooner or later, put me in a hospital or a nursing home. What use is prayer? I see no point in praying."

We pointed to his crutches standing in a corner of his room and said, "Of what use are your crutches if you don't use them!"

Then we prayed with him, prayed him through a Red Sea and around a Jericho. We did not see him again after that visit. John, the beekeeper was, indeed, committed to a hospital by his wife, and died not too much later.

And I, I continue to pray.

There is a story of an old man who had four sons. He loved these sons exceedingly and had brought them up as Christian children should be brought up. They all, however, showed in their adult way of life that they had no desire to love God – to obey any of His commandments. The old man was a praying man, and he spent many hours each day praying for his children. Yet when it came time for him to die, none of his children had been converted. On his deathbed he turned his face to the wall, but unlike Hezekiah, he was not granted an additional fifteen years for more work in his Father's vineyard – for more prayer time for his children's conversion. He was somber as he lay on his deathbed and had no words for his offspring. He did not smile and departed for the next life in quiet reflection. As his four sons attended his funeral, they spoke with one another.

"If indeed our father, who prayed much and was a godly man," said the eldest, "should be so somber on his deathbed, how much more should we, who have lived godless lives, fear God."

The others agreed with him. There was, subsequently, a change in their hearts and lives. It was the harvest of the old man's prayers – a harvest which he never saw – a harvest that was reaped in God's time.

59

Monumental Changes

Therefore prophesy, and say to them, Thus says the Lord GOD: Behold, I will open your graves and raise you from your graves, O My people. And I will bring you into the land of Israel. And you shall know that I am the LORD, when I open your graves, and raise you from your graves, O My people. Ezekiel 37:12-13

My oldest son, Christopher, went with me today to the Stone Center in Waterloo. It is a monument place – that is to say, a place where you can order and buy gravestones. I chose a cross. It's almost four and a half feet high and three feet wide. There were very few crosses displayed in the outside marble warehouse. The proprietor, an agreeable and rotund fellow, drew a picture of what I described.

A strange awareness overcame me – the knowledge that I was buying something that would eventually be broken. In any case, I was not buying something that would last forever. Anco was one for buying solid things. He didn't care for plastic parts and he berated poor quality. Will this stone crack before its time? Will our bodies eventually rise through this particular stone? Will pieces of it fly helter-skelter in the small Bloomingdale Mennonite Cemetery as the souls in the cemetery are reunited with their bodies?

We are to speak of these things. We are to encourage one another as we look forward to the second coming of the Lord Jesus Christ.

I gaze at the sky above Bloomingdale. It is remarkably high and I wonder if everyone on earth will be endowed with a special sort of eyesight at the time of the Second Coming. Will the people in China be seeing what the people in Bloomingdale shall see here? Will all the people in Holland, Belgium, Russia and Thailand see it too? – or will there be a new and different dimension added to everyone's sight?

Will Jesus see all of us individually at the same time? Will I feel this in the core of my being? Will the soul, as it is reunited with the body, attain immediate similarity to Jesus' body? When we rise up, will we sing Handel's "Hallelujah Chorus," or will we be silent, in awe of the majesty of our Redeemer?

Do stones in a graveyard matter? Jesus did actually have a stone placed in front of His grave. And it was rolled away. So perhaps these monuments serve as a reminder that the bonds of death will visibly be broken.

The stone on my parents' grave reads: "Victory through Jesus Christ." Anco's stone, (which is my future marker as well), reads: "We know that our Redeemer liveth." And, at the foot of the monument the inscription continues: "And we will dwell in the house of the Lord forever."

60

Confrontations

Then the LORD said to Moses, "Get up early in the morning and confront Pharaoh as he goes to the river and say to him, 'This is what the LORD says: Let My people go, so that they may worship Me. If you do not let My people go, I will send swarms of flies on you and your officials, on your people and into your houses. The houses of the Egyptians will be full of flies; even the ground will be covered with them. Exodus 8:20-21 (NIV)

As veterinarian Anco was sent up north by the government from time to time. In 2007 he was sent to Coral Harbor where he was stationed for a few weeks. Coral Harbour, is a small Inuit community located on Southampton Island, in the Canadian territory of Nunavut. Anco was sent to this area several times.

During February and March of each year, the caribou herds on Southampton Island are culled and the meat is sold and also used by local people. Anco loved the times he spent up north. He loved the Inuit people and always brought gifts, games such as chess, checkers, etc., to the camp in which he stayed. He initiated conversations and once went to a church service which was conducted completely in Inuktitut. The translator concentrated wholly on him, as he was obviously the only member of the congregation who was not Inuit. Prior to going, he had advised the government that he would not be working Sundays. He wrote in his notebook:

"Gord has offered to cover the kill floor for me today. I'll still do final condemnations where necessary since this is required to be done by the veterinarian. I feel a little odd not working today because we have been down for two days, (there was a storm), but a principle is a principle. I just hope it makes some people think. I'm sure I'll be asked about it tomorrow. May the Lord give me the wisdom to explain in a non-confrontational and yet challenging manner."

He came home with many stories. One story which he recounted to me was about a polar bear. A man, his wife and their twelve-year-old son had gone on a hunting trip. Constructing an igloo as well as a tent on their site, one for living accommodations and one for supplies, they settled in. The man then left his wife and young son at this location to go hunting. During the course of the first day, while he was gone, the wife and son heard a ruckus outside. Cautiously peering out of the igloo, they saw a huge polar bear ransacking the food supply in their storage tent. Because the father had taken all the heavy guns with him, all that the son and the mother had left with which to defend themselves was a small, twenty-two caliber rifle.

Now polar bears are notoriously unpredictable and vicious. But the boy, motivated by a sense of responsibility for his mother, took the small rifle and very quietly and courageously walked up to the bear who was preoccupied with the food. He then shot the huge creature in the ear from close range, the ear being the only vulnerable spot on his body that could effectively be shot at with such a small gun. (The twenty-two-caliber rifle could not have penetrated either the skull or any solid bones such as the ribs or the skull.) As a result of that one shot, the polar bear dropped dead. When the father returned, he was very proud of the fact that the boy had confronted the bear, that he had risked his own life to save that of his mother.

To face a vicious bear head-on, or to confront a brutal problem, is not something many people want to tackle. One of Anco's grandfathers owned a bakery. By all accounts, he was a mild-mannered man and one who very much disliked disagreements. He was a good baker and enjoyed working in his shop. It is recounted that he once saw one of his employees openly steal money from his cash register. Instead of facing and challenging the man, he turned away and pretended that he had not been a witness to the crime. This neither helped the thief nor was of any benefit to himself.

Scripture clearly shows that God does not evade problems. Anco was not one to hide his faith under a bushel. If he perceived that something was askew, he would face that 'bear' and walk up to it with the Bible in his hand. Open thievery from biblical doctrine both angered and saddened him. He never closed his eyes to it; he never tolerated it, even though it cost him dearly at times.

In the fall of Anco's second year at Guelph Veterinary College, he was asked by an older fellow student, also a Christian, if we would like to go with him and his wife to a youth meeting held in Woodstock. The speaker was touted to be very innovative and good. Anco accepted the invitation and we had the couple over for supper. Afterwards we drove with them to Woodstock for the get-together. I can't remember whether or not the gathering was in a church building or not, but do remember vividly that the room designated for the talk was packed with university students. We all sat on benches and shortly after we arrived a bearded man fraternized his way around the room. He was a jovial fellow, clapping students on the back, making small talk while he did so. Eventually, he took his place behind the podium and began his 'talk'.

"First of all," he said, "I want everyone here to feel free to smoke. I know that many of your parents don't want you to smoke, but hey, you're not at home here and I won't tell."

There was a small amount of cheering.

"Also," he went on, "I want you to feel free to say anything. You can discuss any topic you like. This is a free zone."

Anco and I were both beginning to feel slightly uncomfortable. The fellow talked on and on but there was no real topic, only parent-bashing and a mocking of authority. In the long run, jokes were told – inappropriate jokes and loud laughter erupted from time to time. Only we weren't laughing and I whispered to my husband that I thought we should leave. The youth pastor, suddenly extremely aware that we were not laughing along with the others and that we were whispering, centered us out.

"You there," he called out, "What's your name."

I squirmed uncomfortably and looked down. Anco, however, answered.

"Anco Farenhorst."

"Well, Mr. Anco Farenhorst," he taunted, "I notice that you're not amused at my jokes. Why is that?"

There was now dead silence around us and I was afraid. Then Anco aimed his twenty-two-calibre rifle, a rifle named 'Truth', right at the man, and targeted the speaker's conscience.

"Because what you're saying is not funny and it's improper."

Then he stood up, took me by the hand and we walked out.

61

So That We May Be Able To Comfort

Blessed be the God and Father of our Lord Jesus Christ, the Father of mercies and God of all comfort, Who comforts us in all our affliction, so that we may be able to comfort those who are in any affliction, with the comfort with which we ourselves are comforted by God. 2 Corinthians 1:3-4

That you will sooner or later die is a practical and useful thing to think about. What you believe in your heart about death is an important matter to consider, for it will result in either assurance or anxiety; and in whether or not you will be able to offer comfort to others.

Anco and I have had the privilege of sitting at many bedsides, and have been allowed to witness to a number of people drawing their last breaths. Eleventh hour stories are remarkable. They show that it is entirely God's prerogative as to Whom He will have. It is our responsibility to pray – to pray fervently for those who do not seem to know the Lord.

A number of years ago, we had some very dear friends. They were older folks who had immigrated from Holland later in life and who had settled in Owen Sound because they had children there. I first saw this couple in Walmart and heard them speaking Dutch as they were waiting at the checkout counter. Addressing them in their native tongue, they were both surprised and happy to meet someone who was also from Holland. On the spur of the moment, I asked them over for supper and they came.

It turned out that Mr. and Mrs. W were wonderful people, people who endeared themselves to our children and ourselves by their friendliness and unselfish attitude. They babysat and brought warmth and laughter to our family; as a matter of fact, they epitomized what Christian life should mirror in all of its virtues. One thing was lacking, however, and that was that they were never anxious to discuss Jesus Christ. Every one of us loved Opa and Oma W and prayed for them. They, in turn, listened amiably to our reading of the Bible and our prayers at suppertime, but never wanted to discuss personal faith. This was mainly because Mrs. W, without fail, routinely changed the subject.

In the early 1990s, Mr. W was stricken with cancer. We visited him in the chronic care unit of the hospital just prior to leaving for our annual holiday up north. Up to this point, at the venerable age of ninety-one, he had been a vitally alive and healthy person. Knowledgeable about politics, history, chess and woodworking, it had always been a joy to speak with him and he had never been at a loss for words. When we walked into his hospital room, however, like Job's comforters, we could only stand quietly by his bed for the first few minutes. Totally emaciated, he had shrunk into skin and bone.

"Hello, Mr. W."

He opened his eyes, recognized us, smiled faintly and drifted off into morphine-induced half-sleep. We kept talking and every few minutes he would open his eyes and respond with a few words, sometimes sensibly, most often not. When we broached the subject of eternal salvation, he did not seem to be interested. We loved him so much and knew that he would stand before his Maker very shortly. And what would he say?

"Can we pray with you, Mr. W?"

There was a slight motion with the head, indicating agreement. Now during his illness, Mr. W had totally reverted back to his native Dutch, to his mother tongue.

Anco was not fluent in Dutch, so he said, "Well then, Christine will pray with you in Dutch."

Totally shocked, I looked at Anco, but he smiled and nodded at me with perfect confidence, and God gave me the words.

"Lieve Here, Meneer W zal nu wel heel gauw voor U staan want hij is erg ziek. Maar hij wil graag zeggen dat Hij spijt heeft van al de dingen die hij gedaan heeft die verkeerd waren. En hij will graag voor U staan gewassen in het bloed van Christus. En hij wil ook graag zeggen dat hij U lief heeft. Om Jezus wil, Amen." (Dear Lord, Mr. W will very likely stand before You very soon because he is very ill. But he would like to say that he is sorry for all the things that he has done wrong. And he would very much like to stand before You washed in the blood of Christ. And he also wants to say that he loves You. For Jesus' sake, Amen.)

We waited a moment and regarded the parchment face. And the eyes, the eyes that had twinkled at us so often, opened. Suddenly completely lucid, he responded to the prayer.

"Ja, zo is het. Zo is het precies." (Yes, that is the way it is. That's the way it is exactly.)"

Mr. W died about ten days after this visit. A few weeks later, unexpectedly, his wife also died. Although we never saw Mr. W again on earth, I hope that Anco will now have become reacquainted with him in heaven.

62

Reservations

We are confident, I say, and would prefer to be away from the body and at home with the Lord. 2 Corinthians 5:8 (NIV)

Every now and then, usually in the spring, Anco was sent to teach a course in Kingston. It is spring now and I miss these red-letter days. I recall how excited we would become about traveling there. There would be a cosy motel room, and a time of relaxing. After Anco's classes were over in the late afternoon, we'd usually hike, covering several kilometers to do some bird watching in a local conservation area. Then there would be a take-out dinner from a nearby restaurant which we would eat in our motel room. Altogether lovely! But there are no longer any courses now and there is no standing on my head trying to quell the utter exhilaration I always felt prior to a small holiday.

Anco always made reservations prior to these outings. I distinctly remember walking into the motel and having the proprietor lean over the counter, as he asked: "Reservations?"

I would nod and say, "Yes, for Farenhorst."

The man would then check his registry book, run his finger down the columns and stop.

"Yes, here it is – Farenhorst. You're in room seven down the hall."

It gave me a 'taken care of' feeling, a 'chosen feeling' and a confident walk.

Sometimes, a little wobbly on my assurance of salvation, Anco would encourage me, would do a John 14 on me. "Jesus loves you, sweetheart, and I know you love Him. Didn't He say, 'I go to prepare a place for you?'"

This was true and Anco unfailingly underlined the truth for me. For has Jesus not done more than phone for reservations? Did not He Himself actually make a room ready for Anco and myself? Anco is in that room right now – a room more beautiful and cosy by far than our sunroom or any motel room. Jesus had Anco's name highlighted in the registry book and my name is there also, right alongside.

We don't have to pay for that room, Anco and I. It's paid for already!

Perhaps I'll not go to that room the same way Anco went – from a hospital bed. Perhaps the heavens will rend and Jesus will descend from the sky with His angels before I die. In that case, He will call me.

"Christine, come here to Me," He will say, before He escorts me up to that special room He has made ready.

No one will stop me at a desk to ask, "Do you have a reservation?" or "Sorry, we're full up," because Jesus' house has many rooms and one of them is especially for me. 2 Corinthians 5:8 is snugly tucked away in my traveling pocket, in my robe of righteousness, and I am ready to journey home.

PART V:

EYES ON THE HORIZON

63

His Eye Is On

Are not two sparrows sold for a penny? Yet not one of them will fall to the ground outside your Father's care. And even the very hairs of your head are all numbered. So don't be afraid; you are worth more than many sparrows. Matthew 10:29-31 (NIV)

We loved Jack Russell dogs and our first one, Scout, was with us for all of sixteen years. Anco and I both cried when we had to put her to sleep. Almost immediately after she died, we bought another one, naming her Scout number two. We kept this little dog for less than one year, the reason for the short time span being that this second little ball of fire was quite nippy and bit one of the grandchildren.

We happened to know a widow who had recently lost a Jack Russell and consequently gave Scout number two to this lady. About ten years later, this woman telephoned us to say that Scout number two had died and did 'Doc', as she called Anco, know anyone else who might be wanting to sell a Jack Russell? He didn't, but we promised to keep an eye out.

Strangely enough, the same morning as that particular phone call, I stopped by to visit a neighbor. Betsy had been feeling poorly and I was checking to see how she was. Betsy and her husband Bill were not well-to-do. The first floor of their two-storey house had acquired a ground-in dirt accumulation, hiding a wooden floor. The pot-belly stove in the kitchen radiated a perspiring warmth – spring, winter and fall. All the windows of the home were perennially boarded up to keep the warmth inside. It was truly a dark domicile, all the more so because Betsy and Bill were not, at least outwardly, Christians.

Betsy was laying down on the couch when I came in and complained about her sciatica. Her pet dog, a Jack Russell, jumped up on her stomach. Betsy groaned and pushed him away. The animal then came to me, nuzzling my fingers and I suddenly recalled the widow's phone all. Asking if she remembered where she had gotten the dog, I explained to Betsy that I had a friend who wanted to buy one.

"Take this one!" Betsy immediately threw out, "Please take this one!"

"Oh, you don't mean that, Betsy," I replied, "You love your dog."

"Not any more I don't," she insisted, "He keeps jumping on my stomach and it's murder on my sciatica."

"Well," I responded, "if you really mean it, I'll phone my friend and ask if she'd be willing to take it off your hands."

It satisfied Betsy and, to make a long story short, the widow drove down from Owen Sound a few days later, and picked up Polly, Jack Russell dog number three. Encrusted with dirt, Polly's white coat was caked and hard from living with Betsy and Bill. But she was a friendly dog and a good washing worked wonders. Everyone seemed happy.

Betsy was admitted to the hospital a few days after Polly left.

"They think it's a bad infection, something called C. Difficile," her daughter informed me when I called, "and very contagious."

After Betsy was discharged from the hospital, a week or so later, I visited her again. Equipped with a nasal cannula in her nostrils to provide extra oxygen, she looked very frail. A hospital bed had been brought in and placed against the side wall of the living room. Betsy was unable to say much. Her breathing was very labored and she pointed to her stomach to tell me she had a lot of pain. Questioning her daughter later in the kitchen, I asked what the doctor's prognosis was.

"Mom's come home to die," the daughter replied, "that's what the doctor said. And she doesn't have the sciatica. She's got a tumor the size of a baseball in her stomach."

Shocked, I went home in a bit of a daze. Anco and I were leaving for an out-of-town wedding in a few days. Consequently, that same evening, we returned to Betsy's hospital bed side.

"Betsy," I said, bending towards her, "you know that I'm going away for a few days. It means that I might not see you again because it could be that you will be seeing the Lord pretty soon."

She nodded, her eyes fixed tightly on my face and not letting go.

"I'm sure," I continued, "that you must be scared. Especially at night, when it's dark and thoughts creep into your mind about dying."

Her eyes never left my face and she was able to gasp out a very hoarse "yes." I thought of the murderer on the cross and of myself. And what are any of us without a Savior?

"If you are sorry for your sins, and if you believe that Jesus died for them, then you don't have to be afraid."

Betsy blinked and nodded again.

"It doesn't matter how big your sins are, Betsy," I repeated, "God will forgive them if you are sorry for them and believe in your heart that Jesus is Lord and that God raised Him from the dead. Do you believe this?"

Her hoarse "yes" was audible and she would not let go of my face. I told her about heaven where there would be no more pain, or sorrow, or tears. She ate up those words. And then I took hold of her hands and prayed with her, repeating many of the same words. Husband Bill sat in a wheelchair, next to Anco at the foot of the bed.

The strange thing was that Betsy's oldest daughter, a child who had been taken away by Social Services many years previous, was also named Christine. Did Betsy see her daughter in me? Or, another thought to ponder, do all our neighbors see daughters and sons of Christ in us?

We prayed for Betsy in church the next day and she died early on Monday morning.

In a wonderful providence, showing God's care over animals, Polly, the little Jack Russell, found a home prior to Betsy's death. If a home had not been found for her, she would have been grossly neglected or euthanized.

These things are a comfort to me, even now years later. For in such happenings Jesus calls out exclaiming my worth also: Are not two sparrows sold for a farthing? And not one of them shall fall to the ground without your Father's will. But even the hairs of your head are all numbered. Fear not, therefore, you are of more value than many sparrows.

64

Great Promises

His divine power has granted to us all things that pertain to life and godliness, through the knowledge of Him who called us to His own glory and excellence by which He has granted to us His precious and very great promises, so that through them you may become partakers of the divine nature, having escaped from the corruption that is in the world because of sinful desire. 2 Peter 1:3-4

Anco and I used a number of bookmarks in the various books we were reading. We put them there to show us where we had stopped. With Anco gone, I keep up the bookmark habit and continue to read a little each day in various books of the Bible and chapters of devotionals. I find that every time when I begin a passage in the Bible where I left off the day before, that the Lord has a specific message for me.

It was a difficult waking this morning. The sun was seemingly slow in rising and the space next to me in bed glaringly empty. The sparrows fluttered about on the planter outside my window in pairs and I could not grasp the promise, "Weeping may tarry the night but joy comes in the morning." My first Bible passage was Jeremiah 41 – a rather gruesome section where Ishmael murders the governor who was set over the exiles who were left in Israel. Then Ishmael, in turn, is killed and the survivors make the ungodly decision to flee to Egypt. There are so many sins bound up in this chapter, so many heinous crimes committed, it is depressing. If I feel any comfort, any affinity with these events which I can apply to my own life, it is that everything seems so wrong. I can readily empathize because it seems to me on this grey morning that everything in my life has been murdered. In point of fact, it seems perfectly normal to me that I also must flee although I'm not sure where I ought to go. Admittedly, I know that Jeremiah will tell me where to go in the next chapter, but I'm not there yet.

Profoundly pondering, I turn to my next bookmark, to my next passage. It is 1 John 2 – a warning against antiChrists – a warning against anything and anyone who does not accept the Son. It is an exhortation to stand fast in Jesus.

My last bookmarked passage is John 14:1-6. "Let not your hearts be troubled. Believe in God, believe also in me. In my Father's house are many rooms..." These verses tell me that I know more than the vast majority of the people around me. They tell me that today is yet another step towards heaven. They tell me that even though my heart and mind do not comprehend the pain and misery which trouble me presently, my heart and mind are nevertheless enveloped in a breathtaking, holy bear hug and are indwelt by the Spirit.

Three passages – sin and misery, exhortation to stand fast, and hope and fulfilment.

Jesus is my bookmark.

65

Prolonging Life

The fear of the LORD prolongs life, but the years of the wicked will be short. Proverbs 10:27

A number of years ago, Anco and I tried to destroy several huge anthills situated in the back of our property. The red ants who lived there bit hard and their bites were quite painful. Perhaps our zeal to destroy the home of these soldier-like marchers came from the fact that we were surprised in bed one night by a few of the ants. The strange matter was that we lived in a two-storey brick house and our bedroom was on the second floor. Initially, we were convinced that the busy creatures crawling on my nice, white sheets, had been carried in on our clothes. However, when we discovered a dozen or so ants perambulating on the dresser a few days later, we began to search the floor. This search culminated in our finally locating where these little animals had infiltrated our personal abode. We discovered a tiny, almost imperceptible, hole in the corner of the outside wall of our bedroom.

The entire experience was distressing, but it was also fascinating. We stood outside and craned our necks to observe these little, red guys trudging up our brick wall. We watched them until they reached our bedroom window, then saw them disappear through a minuscule porthole. This porthole was invisible to our eyes but very apparent to their compound eyes. Once inside, they marched with precision in one long line through a nap groove in the carpet. Following one another without stepping out of line, they headed for our dresser. Up the dresser leg, up its wooden side, up they climbed onto the top of the furniture. From a distance, the long row of ants looked harmless and cute. But close up, their powerful mandibles were capable of grasping, cutting and biting. As well, their abdomen was capable of emitting formic acid for defense. There, next to some knick-knacks and my jewelry box, they nosed around with nervous speed, eventually partaking of some sweet ant killer we had placed there for their consumption. Then they formed another row and steadily traipsed down the dresser. Neatly, again in one single column, they efficiently hurried back through another line in the carpet nap, a street returning them to their tiny hole in the wall. It truly was incredible to surveil and surveil it as Anco and I did. The little predators were bent on destroying our dresser. Therefore, incredible as they were, we sprayed the hole with Raid. That was the end of them – in our bedroom, that is.

Anco and I visited Belgium in the 1990s. Staying in Antwerp for a few days, we roamed innumerable, tiny streets at leisure. At one point, enamored by the beautiful, stone sculptures manifest underneath the arches of many of the gabled roofs, we slowly walked with our necks craned upward, paying little attention to where we were. As a matter of fact, we were so enraptured by the chiseled carvings over our heads, we did not notice that we had wandered into the red-light district. This came to our attention only after we heard a sharp rapping on the window of one the houses we were passing. Abruptly our gaze dropped down from the high arches to eye level and we were horrified to see a woman, scantily clad in a red dress, smiling and waving at us. She then crooked her finger at Anco, waggling it, inviting him to come in. Reclining in a rocking chair, she sat directly behind the windowpane. We suddenly became aware that the entire street into which we had strolled held numerous windows – bay windows behind which scores of similarly appareled women sat. Holding hands, we began to run and as we ran, we could sense their laughter chasing us. Like the ants who had taken advantage of our unguarded wall, these women had entered the privacy of a chamber meant only for us. They were bent on destroying the water from our cistern, on fouling the water from our well. We ran because we feared – because we feared the Lord.

Proverbs 10:27 tells us that the fear of the Lord prolongs days, but that the years of the wicked shall be shortened. If there is a fear of something which takes away the glory and full majesty of God, if there is a fear of something which diminishes His power and might, and if there is a fear which undermines His promises to His people, then that fear is one which will prolong days.

66

Occupation with Joy

Behold, what I have seen to be good and fitting is to eat and drink and find enjoyment in all the toil with which one toils under the sun the few days of his life that God has given him, for this is his lot. Everyone also to whom God has given wealth and possessions and power to enjoy them, and to accept his lot and rejoice in his toil—this is the gift of God. For he will not much remember the days of his life because God keeps him occupied with joy in his heart. Ecclesiastes 5:18-20

During most of my married days, when I woke up, Anco would already be awake. I suppose that was partly because when he worked regularly, he had to be up early. Anco, however, would not only be awake, but he would also be looking at me. And when I opened my eyes, he would smile at me.

"Good morning, and how is my sweetheart this morning?"

And I would snuggle against him and yawn. What a blessed memory that is! It is a secure memory and I hold it with care. It is an occupation that gives me joy in my heart.

Revelation 1 was part of my devotions this morning. My father frequently opened church services with the greeting from Rev. 1:4b-5: "Grace to you and peace from Him Who is and Who was and Who is to come, and from the seven spirits who are before His throne, and from Jesus Christ the faithful Witness, the Firstborn of the dead, and the Ruler of kings on earth." This morning my day was begun with that greeting. That was an occupation with joy also. John, exiled in Patmos, was alone, but through God's grace he personally wrote to me this morning. The apostle looked at me and said, "Christine, you are blessed if you read aloud the words of this prophecy, and you are blessed if you hear and keep what is written in it, for the time is near" (Rev. 1:3).

The time is near? And I read on: "Behold, he is coming with the clouds, and every eye will see him, even those who pierced him, and all tribes of the earth will wail on account of him. Even so. Amen." A vast expanse of sky is visible through my window pane, and my sins slide past from East to West. And through John's eyes I behold my Lord Jesus, the Alpha and the Omega, the One Who is, Who was and Who is to come – and my heart yearns within me.

I cleaned our back porch this morning and also stained three of the flower boxes which Anco made for me in Arthur. Then I turned the soil in the garden bed behind the porch and trimmed several trees. They were difficult tasks. They were not difficult in and of themselves, but they were difficult because every spring Anco and I would do them together. And now I do it alone.

"Look, sweetheart," I say, "how tall the rose of Sharon has grown!" and "What do you know, the grapevines made it through the winter."

And I see Anco nod and smile. We got the rose of Sharon from a friend who was nicknamed 'Farmer'. Farmer died a few years ago. No one here knows Farmer.

"Should I trim the forsythia?"

In my mind, Anco says 'no'. I knew I shouldn't trim it, but I just wanted to hear him say it in my mind. Then I tell him we've ordered some cedars to plant in a row by our side of the road.

"It's only April," I chat on, "but it's in the eighties today."

And then I cried because I knew I was talking to myself. The dog nuzzled my hand and I blew my nose into the gardening gloves. But the life and the joy God gave us is a good memory and an occupation with joy. Solomon whispers to me over the centuries. "The memory of the righteous is a blessing" (Prov. 10:7a).

Then I remembered the first garden we ever had. It was in Chesley. Anco dug it out from pure grass sod, a back-breaking job. It was a large garden – about forty feet by thirty feet. He borrowed a rototiller after the digging to turn the soil. Then I planted – beans, corn, beets, peas, carrots, onions, leeks and flowers. It was a challenge because my mother-in-law thought my thumb was a failure and certainly not green.

Milly, our neighbor in Chesley, was a perfectionist, a no-weed gardener. There was no fence, so the contrast between our two gardens was blatantly apparent. I could tell that Milly, a squat, short little lady, with more than a hint of moustache, was unhappy with my efforts. Her black eyebrows lifted in a disdainful manner whenever she leaned on her hoe and contemplated our section. Then she would plod over to tell me how satisfying it was to weed. Her husband was an undertaker and I wondered what she used for fertilizer.

Milly knocked at the door one morning, bright and early, carrying some strawberries in a basket.

"Would you like some strawberries?" she asked, her square teeth smiling at me.

Immediately I felt that I had misjudged her and my conscience smote me that I had been irritated with the immaculate, unsullied rows of her vegetables.

"Sure," I answered, "I'd love some."

She came into the kitchen and put a pint of berries on the counter. I visualised dessert and Anco's pleased face.

"Would you like one pint or two?"

Milly was still smiling and I was bowled over by her kindness. But after all, we were still rather new to the neighborhood and this was likely a welcome wagon gesture.

"Two," I said, and tried not to feel greedy, "if it's no trouble."

"No trouble at all," she replied, as she set the second pint on the counter, "and that'll be four dollars."

"Four dollars?"

I paid Milly, disillusioned with the concept of neighbors.

Milly asked me to visit her house one morning. I can't remember why. The rather shabby state of her furniture surprised me. We sat in the kitchen and had some tea. Then Milly asked me if I wanted to see her basement.

"Sure," I agreed and down to the basement we descended. She ushered me into a large recreation room. It smelled new – it smelled so new you could almost taste it. The whole room was covered with see-through plastic. Chairs, coffee table, couch, end tables and what have you all – everything was covered with a Saran-like wrap. Little rows of furniture, no weeds between, stood immaculate and unused.

"How do you like it?" Milly wanted to know, obviously proud.

"Do you sit on the plastic?" I asked.

"No," she immediately rejoined, her eyebrows shooting up, "I'm keeping it neat. Harry and I eat upstairs and don't use this room."

Milly and Harry went to the United Church, but Milly did not like to speak of her faith. Like the furniture in the basement, she kept it wrapped in plastic.

I ponder now whether I keep my joys under plastic, or whether or not people can actually use my joys. For God's gifts to me have been numerous – too many to count – and surely the sharing of them should be obvious.

67

Doing Well

If you really fulfill the royal law according to the Scripture, "You shall love your neighbor as yourself," you are doing well. James 2:8

Sometimes when I pass places, I see myself. For example, when I drive through Guelph, and travel by our former apartment, I can literally notice my face at the old bedroom window; at the train overpass close to our old home, I can detect a young woman pushing a baby buggy with Emberlee in it; and numerous times by the side of the road, I can distinguish the figures of Anco and myself laughing, doing or saying something long forgotten. These pages from bygone days pop up for some unexplainable reason.

Occasionally I wave at myself; at other times I speak; and every now and again I have a great desire to walk in and redo a scene, a moment or a conversation. And I remember that a thousand years in God's sight are but as yesterday when it is past, or as a watch in the night. I recall that God sweeps them away like a flood, that they are like a dream, like grass that is renewed in the morning.

A number of years ago, Anco and I stopped at the old parsonage in Fruitland, at the home where my Dad and Mom used to live. Again I saw a documentary of our yesterdays and wished somehow to recapture some of the moments. While Anco parked the car in the church parking lot and proceeded to take a nap, I walked up to the front door and rang the bell. There was no answer. I then tried the breezeway door.

Knocking and ringing the bell for some time, I was about to leave when someone did answer the door. It was an older lady and she was a bit unkempt. Indeed, the whole exterior of the house appeared rundown and sadly neglected. My Mom had taken great pains to grow fine roses by the front door, but these flowers were now wild, unruly and full of weeds. The grass on the lawn had not been mowed for some time and the hedge, the hedge through which I had walked as a bride, was untrimmed.

"Yes?" the woman addressed me in a neutral sort of voice.

"Hi," I answered, "I used to live here a long time ago. As a matter of fact, I was married from this home. So when my husband and I were passing by, we thought we'd just stop and ... and say 'hi.'"

The woman's demeanor, which had been one of disinterest, softened somewhat. She half-smiled and blinked. She was wearing a housecoat.

"I'm sorry," she spoke softly, "I'm ill and not feeling well."

When I expressed immediate sympathy and interest in her illness, she opened up a bit. It turned out that the terry-robed woman living in my old parental home had cancer – had cancer and did not expect to live much longer. I was very moved. My mother had died of cancer. Did the lady go to church? Was she a Christian? Did she know the Lord? All these questions passed through my mind very quickly. But there was this inescapable truth – living in the erstwhile home of my past, she had now been pushed into my present.

Speaking to the woman about some natural remedies I had explored with my Mom, she became more receptive. And then I told her about a sure spiritual remedy to be employed for cancer of the soul – an illness to which we were all subject. Although noncommittal, she seemed quite grateful. And I hugged her, hugged her close in that very same spot where Anco had been standing when I had knocked on the window to tell him that we were expecting Emberlee. Perhaps this moment was also the beginning of a new birth.

Back in the car, Anco and I prayed for this no-name lady. There are many no-name encounters. "Love does no wrong to a neighbor; therefore love is the fulfilling of the law" (Romans 13:10).

68

I Will Deliver You, and You Shall Glorify Me

Call upon Me in the day of trouble; I will deliver you, and you shall glorify Me. Psalm 50:15

There is not one person in the whole world who has not, at some time or other, been touched by suffering of some kind. Hospitals constantly minister to asthma, cancer and heart-disease patients. Children in all walks of life have to deal with broken families and abuse. Nations are subject to famine and war. Suffering is not really a difficult concept to grasp. It is everywhere. It stares us in the face not only when we sit on our couches watching the national and local news, but also when it nudges us in our personal family and church life. No, suffering itself is not a difficult concept to believe.

There are times in the evening and in the morning when my desire to die and to leave this world with all its problems and pain is very real. My existence at such moments seems to revolve around loneliness. There are sounds, actions and thoughts which only re-enforce anxiety. But in the distance, the far distance, I always hear these words, these comforting words: "Call upon me in the day of trouble; I will deliver you, and you shall glorify me."

Charles Haddon Spurgeon wrote a sermon on this text and entitled it his 'Robinson Crusoe' message. In his sermon, Spurgeon relates how Robinson Crusoe was shipwrecked and stranded on an island and was all alone. Coming down with a severe fever, there was no one to comfort him. He did not even have the consolation of a cup of cold water. Close to death, Crusoe, forced to reflect on past sins, turned to a Bible which he found in a chest. After reading the passage from Psalm 50:15, 'Call upon me in the day of trouble; I will deliver you, and you shall glorify me', Crusoe prayed, prayed for the first time in his life. And after that prayer he felt hope well up within himself.

Pastor Spurgeon goes on to relate that Defoe, the author of *Robinson Crusoe,* was a Presbyterian minister, and that it had been his intent in the book to describe someone in despair of finding peace because of his lack of God. Defoe used Crusoe's reading and praying of Psalm 50:15 to impress this on his readers. He scanned his congregation keenly at this point and observed earnestly that, although Crusoe was not present in the audience, most certainly someone like him was – someone crushed, poor, helpless, and friendless – someone in need.

I readily acknowledge that I am often in need – crushed, poor, helpless and troubled – and I also readily acknowledge that without problems I might become less dependent on the Word of God.

When we are pushed off a cliff, whether that cliff is war, cancer, a snub by a friend, the death of a mother, being maligned and slandered for standing up for the truth, or suffering a stroke – it is of prime significance to note that God has let this happen so that we can die to ourselves and live for Him. He only works for our good.

Shortly after Anco and I moved to Guelph, the Christian Reformed Church began a program called Evangelism Thrust. Little groups were formed within our local Guelph church and each individual group followed a course designed to help the church grow in number. One of the questions we were asked in the group of which we were a part was, "When and how did you become a Christian?"

The truth was that I could not answer that question. I truly did not know. I could not remember a time that I had not known Jesus. Brought up by faithful parents, it seemed to me that I had always been a child of God. Yet, at the same time, it was clear to me that I had grown in spiritual knowledge during trials in my life. I could discern that certain situations had opened the eyes of my heart more and more to see God's tremendous love for me – and those situations were periods of suffering.

There are those who constantly search for miracles. Nevertheless, to be aware that the light of the knowledge of God has shone in your heart is surely the biggest miracle of all; it is surely the most profound of all things! There are times when I consider myself, like Peter, imprisoned by Herod. Shackled between two guards named loneliness and fear, I am astonished that, in spite of the acute pain of Anco's death, I have been able to sleep. For does He not give His beloved sleep?!! Amazingly, light has been shone into these my remaining days, and doors of hope have opened before me. And I am continually being led by the hand of the angel of God Himself outside the gates of despair.

Praise be the Lord!!

Postscript

> *Then we who are alive, who are left, will be caught up together with them in the clouds to meet the Lord in the air, and so we will always be with the Lord. Therefore encourage one another with these words. 1 Thessalonians 4:17-18*

There are many reading this book who are mourning. The apostle Paul urges Christians to weep with fellow Christians who are sad and troubled – but he urges us to do so as those who have hope. It is a blessing to have hoping Christians around us.

Shortly after Anco died, I struggled to write some things down, but was not able to do so. My thoughts were jumbled, scattered and blew away in tears. One thought that came to me, however, was this. Anco and I were going through various parts of Scripture at different times of the day. One Scripture was Exodus 34:29-35. Anco's bookmark was still nestled between the pages of the Bible in that place.

> When Moses came down from Mount Sinai, with the two tablets of the testimony in his hand as he came down from the mountain, Moses did not know that the skin of his face shone because he had been talking with God. Aaron and all the people of Israel saw Moses, and behold, the skin of his face shone, and they were afraid to come near him. But Moses called to them, and Aaron and all the leaders of the congregation returned to him, and Moses talked with them. Afterward all the people of Israel came near, and he commanded them all that the LORD had spoken with him in Mount Sinai. And when Moses had finished speaking with them, he put a veil over his face.

> Whenever Moses went in before the LORD to speak with Him, he would remove the veil, until he came out. And when he came out and told the people of Israel what he was commanded, the people of Israel would see the face of Moses, that the skin of Moses' face was shining. And Moses would put the veil over his face again, until he went in to speak with Him.

Those first days I was so longing to feel, to touch and to see Anco's face just one more time. But the truth was that at that point his face would have had the same shining texture, the same radiant glow, that Moses had. For my dear one, my beloved Anco, was beholding and speaking with His Savior. If at that point in time, while we were still in our earthly bodies, we actually could have seen him, we would have been so struck in awe with the beauty of his face that we would not have been able to bear it.

We had a closed casket. There was a picture of Anco on the casket – a picture which represented him with a smiling and loving face. But, oh, even if that smile and that earthly joyfulness had been increased by a million, we would still not have come close to measuring the fulness of delight with which he is now clothed. We could not and cannot fathom it. We cannot even come close to envisioning it.

I do know this. If Anco were here and able to speak with any person reading this book, he would urge every single one of them, "Oh, taste and see that the LORD is good! Blessed is the man who takes refuge in him!" (Psalm 34:8). And he would go on to say to everyone, "I urge to you confess your sins, and to believe in the Lord Jesus Christ. For whoever believes in him, will not perish but will have everlasting life."

May the Lord have blessed you through the remembrances of this book. May the Lord make His face shine upon you all and be gracious to you; may the Lord lift up His countenance upon you all and give you peace.

Christine

1 Peter 1:24, 25a: "Having purified your souls by your obedience to the truth for a sincere brotherly love, love one another earnestly from a pure heart, since you have been born again, not of perishable seed but of imperishable, through the living and abiding word of God; for all flesh is like grass and all its glory like the flower of grass. The grass withers, and the flower falls, but the word of the Lord remains forever."

Imperishable

Grass withers
In the sun,
Just begun
Softest green
Now is done,
Now has been.
Flowers wilt
As the grass,
Soon they pass,
Soon they fade,
Die *en masse,*
Disarrayed.
Vanity –
All has been,
We have seen
Nothing new,
Common scene
All we do.
Look about,
And survey,
Hair grows gray.
Sunsets glow
On the way
That we go.
Mourners weep
In the street.
Weary feet

Stepping to
Weary beat,
Nothing new.
Vanity –
All has been.
We have seen
Once begun
Softest green
Now is done.

______
God is.

Christine Farenhorst

Also available from Christian Focus Publications ...

978-1-84550-563-9

Afterwards I Knew

Stories from the First and Second World Wars

Christine Farenhorst

From the depths of history and the terrible days of the Great Wars we read stories of courage and danger but ultimately of faith, hope and love. A grandfather sits in front of a warm fire as the flames rekindle memories of times long gone – the next generation needs to know the truth. A table cloth and a large mischievous dog bring two women together from different sides of a bitter struggle. The dominion of Canada and battle scarred Dresden are reconciled through the love of Christ.

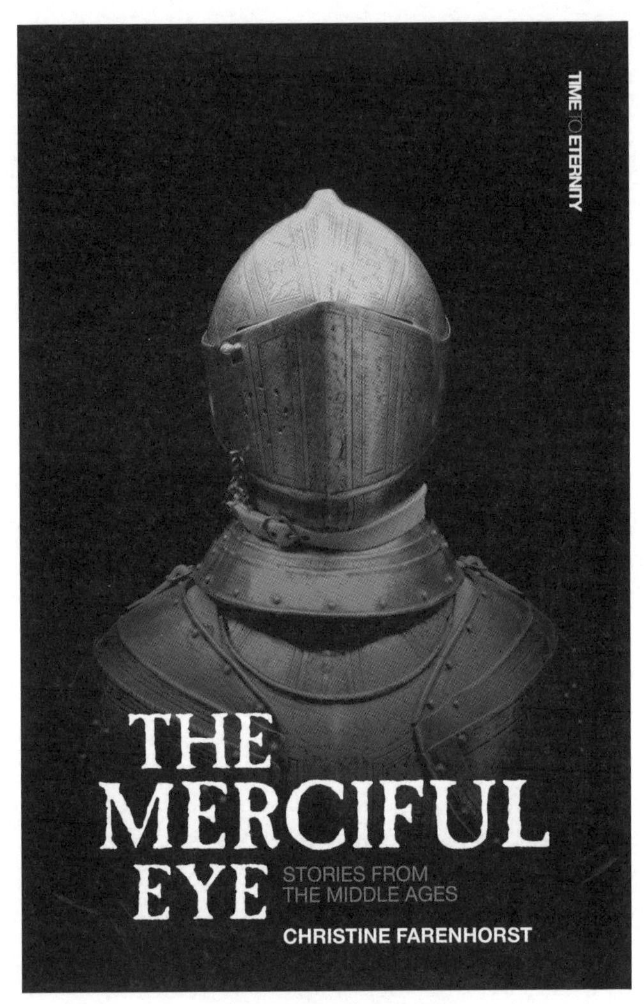

978-1-84550-563-9

The Merciful Eye

Stories from the Middle Ages

Christine Farenhorst

From the depths of history and the dark days of the middle ages we read stories of danger and intrigue but ultimately of faith, hope and love. Jacques hoards his gold but has yet to find real treasure. The young Delia is in danger of being disgraced and unloved... but there is the corner of a garment ready to cover any shame and an eternal heart that beats for her.

There is a strength, beauty and simplicity to the descriptive prose that carries readers into the lives of the characters during living during the tumult of war, with ethical decisions to make. While based in history, the stories themselves are fictional, easily read and profitably digested, and providing food for soul.

CHRISTIAN RENEWAL

Christian Focus Publications

Our mission statement

Staying Faithful

In dependence upon God we seek to impact the world through literature faithful to His infallible Word, the Bible. Our aim is to ensure that the Lord Jesus Christ is presented as the only hope to obtain forgiveness of sin, live a useful life and look forward to heaven with Him.

Our Books are published in four imprints:

CHRISTIAN FOCUS

Popular works including biographies, commentaries, basic doctrine and Christian living.

MENTOR

Books written at a level suitable for Bible College and seminary students, pastors, and other serious readers. The imprint includes commentaries, doctrinal studies, examination of current issues and church history.

CHRISTIAN HERITAGE

Books representing some of the best material from the rich heritage of the church.

CF4KIDS

Children's books for quality Bible teaching and for all age groups: Sunday school curriculum, puzzle and activity books; personal and family devotional titles, biographies and inspirational stories – because you are never too young to know Jesus!

Christian Focus Publications Ltd,
Geanies House, Fearn, Ross-shire,
IV20 1TW, Scotland, United Kingdom.
www.christianfocus.com